Adventure in the Movies

General Editor SHERIDAN MORLEY

Adventure in the Movies

IAN CAMERON

Crescent Books · New York

517 115417

Copyright © Text Ian Cameron MCMLXXIII
Library of Congress Catalog Card Number 73-81193
All rights reserved

This edition is published by Crescent Books
a division of Crown Publishers, Inc. by
arrangement with Roxby Press Limited

First printed 1973
Reprinted 1974

Made by Roxby Press Productions
55 Conduit Street   London W1R ONY
General Editor   Sheridan Morley
Assistant Editor   Bettina Tayleur
Picture research   John Kobal
Design & art direction   Dodd & Dodd
Printed and bound in Spain
by Novograph S. L. and Roner S. A.
Ctra. de Irún, Km. 12,450. Madrid-34
Dep. Legal: M. 4.224-1974

The brief to write a book on Adventure and the Cinema can be interpreted in any number of ways. As adventure movies do not form a neatly definable genre, the one approach which seemed unrewarding was the straight historical survey. Instead I have tried to use the central theme of adventure as a peg on which to hang an assortment of observations about the cinema. The problem of writing in a general way about the cinema is the medium's combination of vast output with (for an art form) a very short timespan: so much has happened simultaneously that almost any generalization works only for a narrow sector of production – one only has to stray slightly outside this sector to be overwhelmed with exceptions. The book's tentative conclusions need to be seen within these limits.

A number of sections are adapted from articles by me in *Movie*; the interview material with Richard Brooks and Howard Hawks is also taken from *Movie*. Books quoted are 'Film as Film' by V. F. Perkins, 'The Best Remaining Seats' by Ben M. Hall, 'Allan Dwan' by Peter Bogdanovich and 'Politics and Film' by Leif Furhammer and Folke Isaksson.

Ian Cameron

FOREWORD BY **DOUGLAS FAIRBANKS JR** KBE DSC

From the earliest silent days through the spectacular 'classics' produced by my father up to and beyond roughly half a century of others (including a few of my own), to the James Bond series, tales of adventure have been a mainstay of the cinema. Of course, adventure stories as such are not exclusively vehicles for particular types of stars nor for particular settings for plots. Rather are they a kind of spirit by which certain films are able to capture the imagination of vast audiences all over the world.

But it has not been enough for these films merely to be tales of exaggerated but vicariously exciting experiences undergone by sympathetic but largely fictional characters. To provide that element of amused or fascinated escapism the best adventure films must involve their audiences, even if just for a moment, in the 'heart-in-the-mouth' fate of their stories' characters, to cheer at some, to curse others, to laugh at and with all of them, and, in most cases, to encourage each viewer's secret wish that it all just *might* be true and that he, given the chance, just *might* have triumphed over odds as cleverly as the hero or heroine in the film. Few lives are either so drab or so vital and 'glamorous' that they do not welcome, when there is a chance, a persuasive escape into a variety of 'Never-Never-Lands'.

In spite of the increasing sophistication of plots and presentations, of occasionally serious and artistically conceived films with less widely patronized intentions, the adventure film as a genre, whether set in the past, present or future, must I believe, remain the essence of the cinema, of what 'movies' are really all about.

CHAPTER 1

IMAGE AND ADVENTURE

Plasterwork temples to illusion:
The Granada, Tooting
The Gaumont, State

The cinemas reflected on the screen.

Louis Lumière, perhaps the prime contender for the title of 'father of the cinema', may also have been responsible for the statement that the cinematograph was 'an invention without a future'. And in the United States, Thomas Alva Edison, who might from the ratio of greed to vision in his personality be cast as cinema's horrid uncle, failed to go beyond this view. He too saw moving pictures as a novelty with little to offer the investor beyond a quick return from music hall and fairground exploitation.

But even before the nineteenth century ended, screens began to light up with evidence that the cinema pioneers had hit upon much more than a gimmicky elaboration of the magic lantern. The quality which turned celluloid to gold was simple and fundamental. It lay in the very nature of the medium, and quickly made itself known in such efforts as that 1896 sensation, the *May Irwin–John C. Rice Kiss*. This unique quality of cinema is the level of gratification it offers in comparison to the small amount of effort required of the audience. The success of television may be seen in comparable terms: the box provides a degree of gratification in return for virtually no effort.

There are various highly-coloured tales of early reactions to the cinema: spectators ducking at the sight of a train rushing towards them or hollering in fright at their first view of a huge disembodied close-up. The common denominator in all these stories is an automatic acceptance of the image on the screen as being a sort of reality. But we hardly need such folk legends of the

8

cinema's birth to understand the importance of realism: the past eighty years have proved clearly enough that the prime source of the cinema's power lies in the comprehensiveness with which it presents a recognizably real world. Unfortunately, most attempts at theoretical systems of film aesthetics have played down this power or sought somehow to transcend it. One of the more grotesque consequences of efforts to grab for the cinema the desirably Olympian status of 'art' has been an apparent shame at its very nature as a recording medium, an attitude which amounts to a denial of its real strength. In his book *Film on Film*, which efficiently clears away the garbage that has largely passed for film theory, V. F. Perkins quotes Paul Rotha's extraordinary lament that 'perhaps the greatest handicap imposed on aesthetic progress was the camera's misleading faculty of being able to record the actual'.

Most of the cinema's development, though, has been protected from this undertow of critical perversity by a sturdy barrier of commercial success. One of the main drives in film history has been towards maximizing the illusion of reality. Sound, colour and wide-screen processes were not commercial subversions of the art of film, but extensions to the cinema's fidelity as a recording medium and hence to its expressiveness. The introduction of each of these developments may have been a purely commercial enterprise, but their long-term survival alone demonstrates their value to the cinema. Compare the fate of Natural Vision or 3-D, where the inconvenience of the process, not to mention the discomfort of wearing polarizing glasses, outweighed the immediacy that the appearance of solidity brought to the image.

The tycoons of the silent cinema were well aware of the importance of illusion, creating fantastic hothouses in which it could flourish. The great movie palaces of the 20s seemed calculated to extend the exotic worlds on the screen to engulf the audience. Thus the design of a theatre like the 1929 Loew's State in Syracuse, New York, was entirely functional, though not perhaps in a manner that would have been recognized by the contemporary adherents of the Bauhaus. The architect, Thomas W. Lamb, described his creation:

'*The Grand Foyer is like a temple of gold set with colored jewels, the largest and most precious of which is a sumptuous mural. It represents a festive procession all in Oriental splendor, with elephants, horses, slaves, princes and horsemen, all silhouetted against a deep-blue night sky. It is pageantry in its most elaborate form, and immediately casts a spell of the mysterious and, to the Occidental mind, of the exceptional. Passing on into the inner foyers and the mezzanine promenade, one continues in the same Indo-Persian style with elaborate ornamentation both in relief and in painting, all conspiring to create an effect thoroughly foreign to our Western minds. These exotic ornaments, colors, and scenes are particularly effective in creating an atmosphere in which the mind is free to frolic and becomes receptive to entertainment. The auditorium itself is also very much permeated by the Orient, but it is not pure and unadulterated like the foyers and vestibules. It is the European Byzantine Romanesque, which is the Orient as it came to us through the merchants of Venice, those great traders who brought the East and its art back to Europe in their minds, as they brought the cargoes in their ships.*'

Gloria Swanson in a Mack Sennett comedy thriller (1917).
The Strange Case Of Poison Ivy.

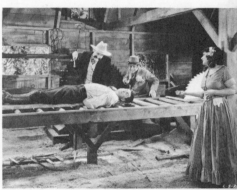

Grace Kelly and Anthony Dawson in
Dial M For Murder **(1954).**

The audience is powerless to intervene...

A film directed by Jean-Luc Godard, *La Chinoise.*

Edward G. Robinson escaping from prison in *Black Tuesday.*

But soon there was to be less need for these plasterwork temples to illusion – creations like the Roxy in New York, which even advertised itself as 'The Cathedral of the Motion Picture'. The illusion on the screen became increasingly self-sufficient, and theatres evolved towards a completely neutral design.

The illusion of reality may be crucial to the cinema, but it is very clearly differentiated from reality itself. For a start, the edges have been removed: we are restricted to a succession of particular viewpoints dictated by the positions of the camera and assembled according to an ever-developing set of conventions. These conventions may be so well accepted as to pass more-or-less unnoticed by the audience, but one distinction from reality is inescapable: in the cinema, we can observe but we cannot participate. Our situation has been nicely summarized by V. F. Perkins:

'We cannot cross the screen to investigate the film's world for ourselves. We are more-or-less impotent in relation to the image because it represents actions already achieved and recorded; it gives us no influence and allows no possibility of intervention or effective protest. But since it is not possible to affect the course of events, it is not necessary either. If we are without power we are also without responsibility. Our exclusion from the world so vividly represented frees us from the need to consider what we see in terms of an active response. We can observe the progress of a fire with that much more attention when it can be neither our business to put it out nor our concern to escape. We concentrate on what we see the more closely because we are not obliged to sacrifice inspection to involvement or flight.'

There is an involvement, though, between spectator and film. Although it cannot grow into any form of intervention, it clearly exists on an emotional level. Presented with recognizable reality on the screen, and unable to join in, we react quite naturally by identifying with one or more of the characters. This identification can be much more than a simple matter of rooting for the good guys; it is susceptible to highly sophisticated manipulation. Much of the moral power of Alfred Hitchcock's films derives from his extraordinary skill in switching our identification from one character to another. Take, for instance, the honeymoon sequence of *Marnie*. We are aware that Marnie is frigid, and we have been encouraged to identify with her to the point of complicity in her stealing. Yet it is with her husband, Mark, that we identify on the wedding night. While she is in the bathroom getting ready, we wait expectantly with him as he nervously fixes drinks. Faced with the provocation of a nightdress which even covers her arms to the wrists, we are still with Mark as he rips off the offending garment. We can maintain this identification as he shamefacedly covers her with a bath-robe, but it is shattered by huge close-ups of him pressing her down on the bed. We are forced to see the meaning of the experience for Marnie. Just as we automatically accept the content of film images as reality, so we cannot help identifying. So strong is this reaction that we can be persuaded to adopt a completely detached position only if we are provided with constant signals of unreality, such as those that puncuate the films of Jean-Luc Godard.

The chariot race from the 1960
Ben Hur.
The Last Days Of Pompeii.
The Longest Day.
Taras Bulba.

Angie Dickinson in
The Sins Of Rachel Cade.

Viveca Lindfors and Errol Flynn
The New Adventures Of Don Juan **(1948).**

Charlie Chaplin and Eric Campbell
Easy Street **(1916).**

The cinema's relationship to its consumers, then, is not at all the same as that of the older narrative forms of the novel and the play, where an effort of imagination is required of the audience. The cinema does not have to demand this effort; in a sense, the spectator is completely passive. Such a thought would probably cause acute pain to many a cinema pundit, perhaps from some puritanical feeling that what is easy must also be unhealthy or stultifying.

Any event that the imagination can conjure up, the cinema can bring to life with uniquely detailed intensity, and this is precisely what we expect it to do. One of the most frequently repeated nonsense statements in film criticism is that something is all the more powerful for not being shown. This is meant as praise, but could just as well be taken to indicate that the director is unequal to the task of depicting whatever he has opted to conceal from our view. The cinema's capability is for showing: we expect the action to take place on the screen. Stage audiences will not be troubled by a convention in which the major pieces of physical action are supposed to have taken place between the acts; the limitations inherent in the medium make this inevitable. Thus it is acceptable to postulate that the Battle of the Somme has taken place behind the proscenium arch while the audience has been in the bar sipping gin and tonic. But a film such as *Becket*, in which the battles take place off screen, is likely to leave us feeling cheated.

Our attention is held by narrative movies first of all on an emotional rather than an intellectual level. This is why the cinema works so triumphantly as a popular art: it communicates through emotions, behaviour and relationships – the material of human experience. Without alienating its mass audience it can portray situations of great complexity and convey the most subtle nuances of meaning.

However, this is only part of the story behind the success of the film business. What it has been selling is satisfaction. The paying customers go to the movies wanting and expecting to be satisfied in one way or another. A film allows us to enter emotionally into a world made real for us. Because of our involvement in it and our attitudes, whether of identification or of antipathy towards the characters, we can be provided with all manner of emotional satisfaction – satisfaction, what is more, without responsibility and without consequences. The withholding of this satisfaction and our doubts about its eventual arrival can be used against us with great effect. Of course, the survival of any art form or (same thing) entertainment medium depends on what it has to offer its audience, but the cinema is notable for the financial ferocity with which the feedback from the audience makes itself felt via the box-office. The success of any cinematic genre can be examined in terms of the sort of satisfaction it offers the audience, whether it be the weepie, social conscience drama, hard-core pornography or the adventure movie.

The popular press, another medium firmly shaped by public demand, shows an obsession with one form of adventure – feats of skill, strength or endurance; climbing the north face of the Eiger or rowing across the Pacific. Dispassionate analysis of some of these deeds may reveal them to be enterprises of little value to mankind,

whether undertaken for their own sake, for publicity, or simply for money, but this does not seem to detract greatly from their appeal. Such is the public appetite for adventure that even quite gratuitous tests of daring seem to fill a need. The heroes, though, have only a fragile hold on the public imagination, because they appear as paragons rather than people: epic climbing expeditions quickly lose their press appeal when it becomes known that up in the rarified purity of the Himalayan atmosphere the heroes have fallen to bickering.

More usefully motivated exploits are liable to throw up heroes and heroines who can quickly be enshrined in film; such is Juliane Koepcke, the girl who survived alone in the Amazonian jungle after an air crash which killed her mother. Even so, one can hardly see film-makers rushing to celebrate a comparably remarkable feat of endurance by the survivors of another air crash, who kept alive on the snows of the Andes for an incredible length of time after the chocolate ran out by consuming the more nourishing parts of the conveniently deep-frozen corpses around them. But if cannibalism might, however unjustifiably, undermine the heroic qualities of this particular story, the cinema has generally one great advantage over the press in dealing with its heroes. They can be presented first and foremost as people, with their own peculiarities and failings. The film hero who is pure hero and more-or-less nothing else can be guaranteed to be the least interesting person on the screen. Even if the part had not been played by Alan Ladd, it would have been

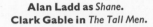
Alan Ladd as *Shane.*
Clark Gable in *The Tall Men.*

**Humphrey Bogart and
Katharine Hepburn struggling
through the swamps with**
The African Queen.
Alfred Hitchcock's *Lifeboat.*

PICTURE PALACES:
**The Astoria, Finsbury Park, London.
The Granada, Tooting, London.**

difficult to work up much enthusiasm for the archetypal Western hero of *Shane*.

Popular journalism always seeks out the human element in a story: the heroism of one fireman is much better copy than the efficacy of team-work by the fire brigade. This principle has repercussions on whatever is being reported: thus politics is seen as a matter of personalities rather than issues. This is only one expression of a general – and easily understandable – concern with people rather than concepts, which is at its most striking in the popular view of history. Here social and political change are passed over in favour of heroes, villains, deeds and battles. All this is meat for the cinema, which is founded on emotional interest. The ideas do not have to be sacrificed to the human story; indeed, the story is the means by which the ideas can emerge.

The cinema, then, is perfectly placed to capitalize on our emotional stirrings of adventure. One can find the quality of adventure throughout the products of the film industry. It is not confined to a particular genre, even if the term 'adventure movie' is used to cover as diffuse a field as the terms 'musical' or 'western'. It is a quality which turns up in almost every sort of story film; indeed the most obvious adventure movies, the sword-and-bosom epics, are usually among the least interesting.

Adventure in the cinema is conditioned by a characteristic of the medium, the minuteness of its gaze. Where a few words or an exchange of glances can add up to a forceful narrative, adventure can exist on a very intimate scale. Opening up the Northwest Passage or the Chisholm Trail is evidently adventure, but so, in the movies, is the discovery of radium, or Glen Miller finding 'the Sound'. The cinema has a facility for turning everything to adventure.

The positive attitude of resistance to social progress as embodied by Jo Van Fleet in *Wild River* (1960).

The search for 'The Sound'
(June Allyson and James Stewart in
The Glenn Miller Story).

17

CHAPTER 2

IMPOSSIBLE DREAMS

Of all the labels that have been applied to Hollywood, none has been more tenacious than that of 'Dream Factory'. The obvious element of truth in this obscures a cluster of misrepresentations. There is, for example, the suggestion of uniqueness in the label. While Hollywood may have been the most efficient dream factory, virtually every other film studio is in the same business. Even the glummest works of Socialist Realism from Stalinist Russia were selling the dream of at least one man – the great leader himself.

And here we come across another problem of the Dream Factory label: dreams are not manufactured in the movies. They may be exploited there, directed, or clothed with circumstantial detail, but the dreams themselves are in the audience, waiting for the movies to satisfy them. So intimate is the cinema's relationship to its public that it is almost a prerequisite for success that a film should realize some dream in the minds of its spectators.

The worst aspect, though, of the Dream Factory label is the undertone of disapproval in it, the feeling that there is something actually harmful in movies as wish-fulfilment. Individual fantasies may be cosy or masochistic, constructive or anti-social, but even the worst of them can be exorcised in the cinema, with an emotional effect that is positively beneficial. Equally, propaganda films have often used audience reactions that would normally be admirable to reinforce the most oppressively totalitarian of messages. It is not the nature of the dream but the way the film uses it which is crucial. Out of the interaction between the dream and its realization emerges an effect which is, in the broadest sense, moral. Any idea that an element of wish-fulfilment is a deficiency would largely rule out the popular cinema as a subject for admiration.

The Russian film, *The Fall Of Berlin*, **with M. Ghelovani as Stalin and M. Goborov as Molotov.**

Wish-fulfilment is a characteristic of nearly all forms of cinema; but it is at its most conspicuous in adventure movies. We have to go right back to the beginnings of the cinema to observe the birth of one form of adventure movie, the fantastic, which brings to life dreams that in reality would be unrealizable, if not actually impossible. In the movies, you can do almost anything: when a wheel comes off Bob Hope's car in the climactic chase of Frank Tashlin's *Son of Paleface* (1952), he uses a rope to support the axle as he drives on. 'Hurry up,' he yells to Roy Rogers, who has ridden off in pursuit of the wheel, 'I've just realized that this is impossible.'

Within a few years of the first Lumière films, in 1896, Georges Méliès, an illusionist with a small theatre in Paris, was experimenting with a movie camera. He first tried filmed equivalents of the conjuring tricks he performed on stage, but before long was using film for tricks which he could never have managed in the flesh: with a carefully framed shot tracking towards a grimacing head, he was able to give the impression of it swelling up like a balloon (*The Man with the India Rubber Head*, 1902). Méliès, though, was more than a virtuoso of camera trickery. At the turn of the century, while his contemporaries were contenting themselves with filming one-minute snippets of actuality, or fragments of theatre or vaudeville performances, Méliès was devoting a large part of his effort to contriving things for his camera to photograph. In a huge output (over 360

19

George Meliés fantasy.

Jean Cocteau's *Orphée* **– fantasy juxtaposed with reality.**

short films in his first ten years of production), the least remembered part of his work is his invented newsreels. In his studio at Montreuil in the suburbs of Paris he staged and filmed the Dreyfus affair, a world congress in China, a volcanic eruption in Martinique and even (before the event) the coronation of Edward VII. At the same time, he was developing his trick films into something more than displays of optical prestidigitation; he was launching the cinema into the realms of story-telling. Before 1900, he had already filmed such standards as Cinderella, William Tell, Joan of Arc, and Christ Walking on the Water. He went on to more elaborate and fantastic creations including *Journey on the Moon* (1902), which can perhaps be described as the first science fiction adventure movie.

Works claimed by the film historians as notable firsts have a way of turning out to be isolated efforts, of no interest beyond the earliness of their production. The Méliès fantasy films, though, were immensely popular and widely imitated; even today, their charm, at least, survives. But the cinema is, with television, the most perishable of the arts, and after seventy years, it is impossible to see these pictures as anything but quaint, even poignant relics from a forgotten past.

It would be unfair to compare Méliès as a visionary with his immediate antecedents in popular literature, H. G. Wells or Jules Verne, even though some of his inspiration may have come from them. For where they were using a medium that had developed over a period of centuries, Méliès was pioneering the technique of telling stories with a gadget that had been around for only a decade. He could occasionally manage well-depicted details – a balloon flying over a realistic Paris, or, in *Journey on the Moon*, the industrial landscape behind the rooftop launching platform. But the narrative in *Journey on the Moon* is a primitive succession of *tableaux vivants* pitched at the level of provincial vaudeville, complete with cavorting chorus girls at the take-off and a sky a-twinkle with female-faced stars. The moon is hit full-face by the rocket, which disgorges its crew of frock-coated worthies in a rocky moonscape which is in considerable turmoil – some sort of geological catclysm is in progress, perhaps provoked by the landing. Amid spouts of steam and small-scale moonquakes, the explorers, looking as if they had taken a wrong turning on their way to a Legion of Honour ceremony, are set upon by the prancing, hairy natives. It is difficult today to discuss a Méliès fantasy film without seeming patronizing.

This tentative joint origin, in Méliès' work, of film fantasy and film narrative might tempt one to the conclusion that fantasy and cinema are natural partners. However, there is little in the history of the cinema to bear this out. The most successful fantasy pictures that come to mind are well outside the popular cinema – Jean Cocteau's *Orphée* and *La Belle et la Bête* – and Cocteau had anyway a particular genius for creating imaginary worlds out of fragments of the real world. In theory, the cinema should be a perfect medium for realizing the visions of science fiction. Somewhere along the line, though, a fatal alliance grew up between science fiction and low budgets. The space serials of the 30s and 40s with, say, Buster

20

Satan's Satellites.

SPACE CHEAPIES
Cat Women Of The Moon.

Buster Crabbe as Flash Gordon.

Crabbe as Flash Gordon were succeeded by the space B-features of the 50s, which had clearly identified the money-saving potential of the genre. Provided that special effects could be kept to a minimum, a few plastic space guns, some winking control panels and a few other items of stylized hardware could disguise a budget cut to the bone: sets could be little more than flats and curtains, while costumes could be economically reduced to para-military simplicity, or even found second-hand. *Queen of Outer Space,* a 1958 cosmic cheapie with Zsa Zsa Gabor in the title role, was in this money-saving league, clothing one of its lesser harpies in a costume that Anne Francis had worn more fetchingly two years before in *Forbidden Planet.*

Science fiction seems to be one of the genres least suitable for low budgeting; there is so much to be done. Vast areas of shared experience can simply be assumed in contemporary or historical subjects, but in building up a science fiction world that is entirely imaginary, the starting point is, in effect, a total blank. Everything has to be created, with the result that any slackness in the conception is cruelly exposed.

So far, there has been little effort by the cinema to penetrate beyond the most elementary levels of science fiction. A few basic patterns account for the great majority of science fiction films – for example the mad scientist movie, which does not qualify for inclusion under the banner of adventure. Nor does the doomsday-threatened, world-defensive science fiction movie, which with a few more interesting exceptions (such as *Invasion of the Body Snatchers*)

Planet Of The Apes **(1967).**

belongs with that most innocuous of forms, the rubber monster movie; the threat is often scarcely more potent. It is linked, though, to the other main science fiction genre, the space adventure, through one standard plotline: 'something is amiss in the cosmos, and fearless cosmonauts are dispatched to investigate', a synopsis which covers works as diverse as *Forbidden Planet, 2001: A Space Odyssey*, and most episodes of *Star Trek*.

Whether the spacemen are out to explore or to investigate, a prodigious amount of construction work is needed. The cinema operates in such a literal mode that it will not accept stylization of settings as an alternative to realistic building. The only space movies where construction is not the central problem are those which can somehow find an excuse for using terrestial locations: Byron Haskin's *Robinson Crusoe on Mars* did a very creditable job using Death Valley for its Martian settings. *Planet of the Apes*, too, after a brilliantly staged space-ship crash, sets its simian civilization in Earth-like surroundings, but then it eventually reveals itself as being less a space movie than a time movie – in a shock revelation of stunning predictability, Charlton Heston finds himself face to face with the Statue of Liberty, and we are meant to be bowled over by this clinching image of a civilization that has destroyed itself.

Most science fiction films fall down before the message has a chance to lumber into view. Either through budgetary inadequacies or through some lapse from fanatical perfectionism in the effects, the spell is undermined. The hypnotic quality of cinematic illusion when

James Carne in *Countdown* – a space movie shot on location in Death Valley!

Studio Antarctic – John Mills and Derek Bond in *Scott Of The Antarctic* (1948).

The Woman On The Moon **(1928).**

Metropolis **(1926) – city of the future.**

23

it is working contrasts with the crippling effect of its failure, which can strike in apparently trivial ways: a memorable example occurred in *Scott of the Antarctic* where the studio scenes were all too evidently not taking place in antarctic temperatures, as there was no condensation of the actors' breath. The space movie is similarly vulnerable at every point, and process work brings with it a new range of hazards from blue outlines to disturbing errors of relative scale.

Only a handful of science fiction films have managed to solve the technical problems which are no more than a qualifying round on the way to success. Fritz Lang, after his success at least on a physical level with a city of the future in *Metropolis*, went on to deal with space flight in *The Woman on the Moon* (1929). It was remarkable

Anne Francis and Robby the Robot in *Forbidden Planet* **(1956).**

mainly for the completely convincing model work and for the staging of the blast-off. Here Lang had a big advantage: his technical advisers were Hermann Oberth and Willy Ley, both of whom became notable figures in rocket technology, Oberth in Nazi Germany, Ley in the United States. The moon, however, is credited with a breathable atmosphere and a surface covered in gold. The plot is a novelettish story of greed and self-sacrifice; there is even a child stowaway.

The most remarkable of all science fiction films is *Forbidden Planet*, which had the resources of MGM behind it, a brilliant special effects man, Joshua Meador, borrowed from Walt Disney for the occasion, and a director, Fred McLeod Wilcox, whose only major success in the past had been *Lassie Come Home*. To some extent, it can be seen as a space version of *The Tempest*, but the parallel, though often drawn, is a fragile one, and the film succeeds very well without any reliance on Shakespeare.

Walter Pidgeon and his daughter, Anne Francis, are the only survivors of a colony established on the planet Altair IV. They live in a magical oasis staffed by a friendly if somewhat lugubrious robot called Robby. Underground there is a huge power source left behind in full working order by an extinct civilization, the Krel. There is also a fearsome but largely invisible destructive force which attacks a space ship which has come to investigate. The camera follows it towards the ship as its invisible feet leave a track of huge footprints in the sand. The creature is revealed as a monster from the Id, an expression of the destructive forces of the subconscious, which exterminated the Krel and is now locked to the mind of Walter Pidgeon, who sacrifices himself to stop the monster and destroys the planet.

Although the effects are worked out with stunning expertise, they are the product of inspired fantasy rather than of scientific prediction (this is a difference of kind rather than of quality). Even the fragmentary description given here is enough to suggest that *Forbidden Planet* has a strong human dimension, which is lacking in most space movies, and that for once, there is thematic substance to match the technical inventiveness.

Puppet space – TV's *Startrek* **and** *Thunderbirds Are Go.*

In general, science fiction differs from other film narrative forms in the insignificance of the characters. We are offered visions of the

2001: A Space Odyssey **(1968).**

The Underwater City **and** *Fathom*, **and in the sky** – *2001: A Space Odyssey.*

technological future; the usual assumption seems to be that for human nature it is going to be business as usual. Hence the people can be relegated to the position of pawns in the prediction game – the level of characterization is not all that much higher in *Star Trek* than it is in the puppet space films of the *Thunderbirds* variety. With characterization reduced to a level where it will not complicate matters, any message can be made to come across loud and clear; there is a temptation to fill the hiatus at the heart of the picture with a Statement. The larger the picture, and the more effort it has required, the more irresistible this temptation becomes, as if the message were the magic ingredient to make it Important. Ultimately, the characters have been sacrificed not to the technology but to the message. The film studios have always tacitly accepted the unimportance of the people – even the largest of science fiction films is unlikely to have in its cast any stars of great box office consequence.

The ultimate in this respect is *2001: A Space Odyssey*, which is so hung up on the hardware that nothing else has a chance: Hal, the computer, displays more personality than either of the leading actors. In both *2001* and Stanley Kubrick's subsequent film, *A Clockwork Orange*, there is (to borrow a phrase from another critic) so much less than meets the eye. An extraordinarily elaborate treatment of the surface detail does not bring with it a comparable richness of intellectual structure. In *2001*, the surface is often very impressive, particularly such things as the interior of the spaceship that is carrying Keir Dullea and Gary Lockwood to Jupiter. The sets and the effects are impeccable. But once one has gasped at the visual mastery, the next response is likely to be a non-committal 'So what?'. There is another snag, shared by a later space movie, *Marooned*, and observable in the real thing, the television transmissions from the various Apollos: out in space, the astronauts move very slowly. As dramatic action, the space movie suffers from the disadvantage of plodding slowness which was always so characteristic of underwater pictures.

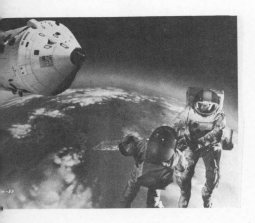

CHAPTER 3

THE GREAT INDOORS

The most effective imaginary worlds Hollywood has created have been terrestial, not science fiction, although they have often been no more real in a documentary sense than Altair IV. The views the movies offered of various exotic locales must have been baffling to the natives. Their incomprehension would not merely have been caused by the glamour their home towns acquired on screen – a degree of improvement is only to be expected in studio reconstructions. Thus Allan Dwan, the director of the 1922 *Robin Hood*, recalled that Douglas Fairbanks 'was always insistent on historical accuracy, though I doubt there was ever a castle as big as ours. But, you see, most castles are disappointing – they're so little . . . most of them are squatty things, and *all* the English castles are unimpressive. Even if I were going to do Windsor Castle, I'd make it bigger and more elaborate.' But the unreality of non-American settings was more than a matter of making them bigger and better: Hollywood was not treating its audiences to souped-up visions of the real Shanghai or Algiers or Istanbul, but to totally arbitrary constructions to which these names had been grafted.

One should not get too hung up on the fidelity of settings to some observable original; what matters in the end is that the world presented by the movie should be believable to its audiences. The richness of a movie like Arthur Penn's *The Chase* is answer enough to those who complain that Texas isn't like that. On the other hand, the daftness of Sam Peckinpah's *Straw-Dogs* would be redeemed hardly at all even if his attempts at capturing 'Cornishness' were to extend beyond 'Mummerset' accents and a chorus of 'Where be that blackbird to?'

To appreciate why documentary accuracy mattered so little for so long in Hollywood, we need to glance at the way the business developed. The first decade of the twentieth century saw the emergence of the movies from the penny arcades into the big time. As the business grew, it acquired the attributes of an industry, and its retail outlets, the movie houses, needed a regular supply of product. This could be provided most reliably by massive production concerns, which soon came to dominate the industry. The ideal conditions for making films – sun and a good range of accessible locations – were to be found in southern California, where the industry became centred, just as the cotton industry had settled in Lancashire or the potteries in Staffordshire. For the giant film production companies which had grown up by the end of the silent era, the most sensible way of working approximated closely to that of any other manufacturing industry. By concentrating production into a studio (i.e. factory), a company could keep the maximum of control, whether budgetary or artistic.

The major studios' control of the film industry was made more-or-less absolute by the arrival of sound, which required a massive escalation of technical resources. Filming became concentrated around the all-important sound stages with their seemingly ideal shooting conditions. At the studios, all the supporting services were on hand, and any scenes which required open spaces could be shot on the backlot, or somewhere nearby – this was the era when directorial wanderlust could expect to be vetoed with the comment that 'a rock

Marlon Brando and Robert Redford in Arthur Penn's *The Chase* **(1966).**

Dustin Hoffman and Peter Vaughan in Sam Peckinpah's *Straw Dogs* **(1972).**

28

Allan Dwan's *Robin Hood* (1922).

Beau Geste (1939) – the American Middle East.

29

Maria Montez in *White Savage* **(1943),**
in *Ali Baba And The Forty Thieves* **(1944),**
with Sabu in *Arabian Nights* **(1942).**

is a rock, a tree is a tree – shoot it in Griffith Park'. The vast facilities available had to be kept in use, for otherwise, as later sad experiences showed, they would be nothing but unproductive overheads and exploitable real estate.

The problems of filming at any distance reinforced the pressure to stay in Hollywood. When travel still meant Super Chiefs and Cunarders, the main factors were transport and communications. A film unit that got far beyond the state line, let alone across the sea, must have seemed to the studio managements like a unit almost beyond control. The 60s heyday of Cinecitta as an expatriate Hollywood was founded on good communications as much as on lower production costs. A vital, if intangible, role in the development of the film industry has been played by transatlantic telephones and jets. But in the days before even the Stratocruiser, the pressures to shoot at the studio were almost irresistible.

So films were made in huge factories by salaried staffs and contract actors. The people who made movies were exposed mainly to contact with other people who made movies. In view of their enormous following, Hollywood movies were produced in remarkable isolation from the world inhabited by their audiences. Insofar as reality obtruded into the industry's creative consciousness, it was an American reality, recognized by the gangster and exposé films which flourished in the 30s. The gang wars of *Little Caesar* (1930), the dapper tough guy exploits of James Cagney in such films as *Public Enemy* (1931) and *Angels with Dirty Faces* (1938), the pseudo Al Capone in *Scarface* (1932) were drawn from the real gangsterism of the era. But outside these established film genres reality was only to be found in such isolated efforts as King Vidor's *Our Daily Bread* (1934) and John Ford's version of *The Grapes of Wrath* (1940). Hollywood's particular brand of isolationism was propelling it towards a picture of the world made up of two countries, the United States and the other place.

Richard Brooks, who later directed *Blackboard Jungle*, *Elmer Gantry* and *The Professionals* started out as a writer in the early 40s. His first assignment was 'a picture with Jon Hall, Maria Montez and Sabu, directed by Arthur Lubin and called, I think, *The White Savage . . .*'.

'Then one day in 1942 I got a call from Universal, a different producer.

He said, "You worked on that picture with those three great actors that we made here. It was a very successful picture."

I said, "I didn't see the picture."

He said, "Well, we have the same three great actors, Jon Hall, Maria Montez and Sabu, but we haven't got a story and we'd like to have a story for them. But it's got to be about a desert."

"Well, there's a desert right here in the United States."

"Oh, no. No Cowboys and Indians, that's out. Name me a desert."

"The African Desert."

"No, that's Foreign Legion, been done to death! Name me another desert."

"Australia."

30

Hollywood's studio constructions . . .

BECKY SHARP

A ROUBEN MAMOULIAN PRODUCTION

Trail Of The Lonesome Pine (1936).

"Well, who's the natives?"

"Australians, I guess. I don't know. What d'you mean?"

"No, no," he said, "you know, the heavies, the natives."

"Let's see, I don't know, there are a number of bushwhackers or something."

He said sorrowfully, to me at any rate, "Any niggers?"

I knew this wasn't my man right away, but I said "Well, there must be coloured people, yes."

"Out! No race problems. Name me another desert."

"China?"

"*The Good Earth*, let's stay away from that."

"How about India?"

"Yes, but nobody's British in this cast. So who're we gonna have? That's politics anyway, lots of trouble in India."

By this time, I'm fast running out of deserts and I said, "What about Turkey? There's a desert there."

"Sounds interesting. Who are the heavies?"

So I said, "Now wait a minute, I don't know the story, I don't know who the heavies are."

He said, "Now I'll tell you what. You go and write the story."

I got some National Geographical Magazines, read up on Turkey and came across a rather interesting aspect. After the First World War, they were trying to liberate the women, and many new customs were coming in, education, getting rid of the veil, and so on. Good for Maria Montez. At least she'd be able to do something in that. I built some sort of story and sent it to him. Two days later I get a call.

"You let me down, boy."

"What's the matter?"

"Well, where are the riffs?"

"The riffs? There are no riffs in Turkey."

"No, no, you don't know what I mean. I mean the fellows in the white sheets on horses."

I said, "No riffs in Turkey."

"You must be crazy. Now, there is a Turkish consul here in Los Angeles. Why don't we call the fellow?"

Next day, a nice young man comes round: black moustache, about 30, 32.

"This is going to be great for your country," says the producer. Every producer says that. "We want to do a story about Turkey," etc., etc. "Who are the heavies?"

"I don't know what you mean."

"Well, who are the natives?"

"Turks."

"I mean, don't you have trouble with people?"

"We're having some trouble right now."

"Who are you having trouble with?"

"Well, we have a tribe called the Kurds, and they are having a kind of little revolt in the desert."

"The Kurds? Sounds kinda dirty."

Back to the National Geographics. I found an interesting aspect.

The technicolor camera on location for *Trail Of The Lonesome Pine*.

When the Suez Canal was being thought about, they had to decide whether it would be a shorter route. So two packet boats left India, one to go round the Horn and the other to, I guess, Port Suez. Then the parcel would be put on a horse and camel and go to Alexandria, then to London. It beat the other boat by three weeks. I thought the section from Port Suez to Alexandria would be interesting. You know, the Pony Express. Sabu could ride a horse. So I wrote it and sent it in. Two days later . . .

"You let me down."

"What's wrong?"

"Where are the riffs?"

I said, "There are riffs in Africa but they're nothing to do with the building of the Suez."

He said, "I'll prove it to you."

And the next day we go to see this movie called *Suez* with Tyrone Power and Annabella. In the second reel, six guys in white sheets drive up and blow the canal.

"So," he says, "you see?"

And he leaves. I sit there and watch the rest of the film and it turns out that these guys weren't riffs but the British masquerading as riffs to blow up the canal because the French were building it. So I go and explain it to him and he says "I'll tell you what, let's call the boss."

. Because, you see, he was only the producer and he had another producer over him.

The Western permanent set!

He said, "Jack, I've got this story here and it's quite good. Perhaps we ought to do a screenplay."

And Jack, who has a very loud voice, the kind you could hear even without the telephone, says, "Well, is there anything for the broad to do?" (He meant Maria Montez.)

"Oh yes, she rides on horses, she rides on camels, clouds of veils, all that sort of thing, it's great. Sabu gets killed and he's very heroic. Jon Hall gets wounded and they get the mail. It's the Pony Express, except that it's in Africa."

And Jack (I won't mention his name), he says, "When does this story take place?"

And I say, "Before the Suez Canal was built, Jack."

Jack says, "When the hell was that?"

And I got up and I joined the Marine Corps.'

Apart from considerations of dodging political trouble, which might result in a film losing an audience somewhere, it made very little practical difference where the story was set, since any brand of exotic atmosphere involved the art department rather than the travel agency. As the cinematic conceptions of all countries came from the same handful of art directors, it was hardly surprising that they wound up exhibiting a degree of uniformity. In the lower budgetary reaches, permanent sets on the studio backlots were likely to be adapted to do duty for a variety of countries. (The permanent sets, though, really came into their own with post-war Westerns, where one film's Abilene was another's Tombstone, and

Humphrey Bogart's bar – with
Peter Lorre in *Casablanca* **(1942)**
and with Lauren Bacall in
To Have And Have Not **(1944).**

each studio had its own, offering the *aficionados* scope for nostalgic exercises in recognition.)

Far-away places, then, tended to receive an identikit treatment, which had the effect of reducing most of them, particularly the non-European ones, to a common geographical limbo. Although the decor was different, the bar which Humphrey Bogart owned in *Casablanca* (1942) was to all intents and purposes the same one that he inhabited two years later in *To Have and Have Not*, except that this time, the setting was Martinique. And indeed it was shot in the same studio: in *To Have and Have Not*, even the fishing boat sequences appear to have been filmed on a sound stage.

No particular year can be pinpointed as the time when Hollywood film-making broke away from the sound stages; studio shooting was never an absolute rule even in the 30s. After the introduction of both sound and colour, ways were quickly found of using the new developments on location – Henry Hathaway's *The Trail of the Lonesome Pine*, which had location shooting in colour, came less than a year after Rouben Mamoulian's *Becky Sharp* (1935), the first feature to be made in three-strip Technicolour.

The principle of going to a place rather than building it gradually became dominant in the 50s and 60s. This shift was, in effect, no more than a change of emphasis in favour of some location shooting – the adventurous Otto Preminger was very much the exception in aiming to shoot even his interiors on location. The experience of documentary shooting which some directors had had with the US Navy and the Signals Corps may have contributed to this change, as well as the rise of the Western from its B-feature eclipse during the 30s. This was a genre which really demanded location work, but often did not get enough of it. The high proportion of exteriors shot indoors undermined Cecil B. Demille's often excellent Westerns and contributed to the fatal lack of conviction in William Wellman's 'serious' Western story of a lynching, *The Ox-Bow Incident* (1943).

Visually, it was colour that made indoor exteriors untenable and ended the career of those amazing painted vistas which stood in for distant views of towns that existed only as façades in a studio. In black and white, these conventions were usually unobtrusive, but living colour made the deadness of the settings all too apparent. The larger the screen, the less acceptable studio contrivances became – *West Side Story* demonstrated the importance of real locations for a 70mm film by falling on its face as soon as it retreated into the studio.

Encouragement for location shooting must have come around 1950 when three-strip Technicolour, which required a cumbersome special camera, was replaced by Eastmancolour, which used the same cameras as simple black and white. In general, transport became easier at the same time as economics were turning against the film studios. It was increasingly more sensible to travel than to construct. The limbos in which movies, particularly adventure movies, had usually been set, were often replaced by real surroundings, a change which had to have other effects. Most obviously, the film-makers were exposed directly to the places they were supposed to be portraying.

37

Location interiors – Eve Marie Saint
and Ralph Richardson in
Otto Preminger's *Exodus* (1960), and
Jane Fonda and Robert Hooks in
Hurry Sundown (1967), also directed by
Preminger.

The real thing – *Stagecoach* (1939) in
Monument Valley.

Thus Richard Brooks, going to Kenya to film Robert Ruark's novel about the Mau Mau, *Something of Value*: 'A best-seller, and when I got to Africa, they got hysterical laughing at me. They were laughing at the novelist and at me for even coming near Kenya with the book. It was trash. Eventually I got what I thought was rather a good script. . . .'

It would be idle to pretend that contact with real locations breathed instant authenticity into Hollywood movies; for every *Something of Value*, there were lots like *Three Coins in a Fountain*. But the change in the patterns of film-making did spell doom for some of the more dated forms of adventure movie – the stories of intrigue and romance set in the mysterious cardboard Orient, and the low-budget desert epics that were one of the staple products of Universal until the early 50s. The last of the desert movies, though not from Universal, was *Timbuktu*, which emerged in 1958, so far out of its time as to be high camp rather than high adventure. With Yvonne de Carlo in a yashmak and John Dehner as a scar-faced sheik whose villainy extended to torturing a British officer by pegging him out under a tarantula suspended on a lowly unwinding ball of thread and then lamenting that the victim had died too quickly to provide any information, this was the movie which produced howls of mirth from the critics with Victor Mature's line: 'I've got the holy man stashed.' Only the copyright date reminds us that the film appeared after the real desert splendours of Henry Hathaway's *Legend of the Lost*. The extraordinary thing about *Timbuktu* is that it appears to have been made completely without self-consciousness. But as a memorial to the old Hollywood, it is much more satisfactory than later films in which the nostalgia has been more calculated.

FILMS SHOT ON LOCATION
West Side Story **in New York.**
Something Of Value, **Rock Hudson in Kenya.** *Legend Of The Lost*, **Sophia Loren and a camel train in North Africa.**

39

CHAPTER 4
PERSONALITY OF THE ADVENTURER

Human nature demands that heroes appear in some way exceptional. Mr Average is nobody's dream man. The film hero – the focus of movie-goers' identification – has to be remarkable, whether for looks, physique, personality, eloquence, wit, cunning, sangfroid, or daring. He need not, of course, exhibit superlative prowess in all these departments, but equally he must not be obviously deficient in any of them – though the less straightforward qualities of wit and cunning are optional in figures who can call upon the folksy virtues of invincible strength or immaculate rectitude. We hardly expect to be dazzled by verbal brilliance from, say, Roy Rogers or Steve Reeves. Indeed, outbursts of slick repartee would probably detract from their uncomplicated character as 'guardians of right'. It has often been remarked that it is the heavies who get all the good lines and seem to have most of the fun, while virtuous heroes remain stoically inarticulate. The allure of the bad guys, which springs in part from our vicarious involvement in activities denied to the law-abiding citizen, can often more than counter-balance our feelings for the good guy. When the heavy was someone as good as Arthur Kennedy or Robert Ryan, the hero really had a tough time winning the audience, even though the rules dictated that he would come out on top in the last reel.

Robert Ryan and Jane Russell in *The Tall Men* (1955).

With a few exceptions, the crucial ingredient that makes major stars is personality. Glamour alone is a qualification only for second-rate stardom. The real eyeful offers merely passing gratification; something more is required to grip our attention. The proportion of college athletes and beauty queens who really made it in the movies is very small.

Breathing vitality into a dumb but glamorous carcase was on the whole beyond the skill of the studio Svengalis – the idea that stars can be manufactured belongs to the mythology of the film business. What the studios were adept at doing was masking the deficiencies of performers who had the necessary star quality but were either too short, too old, too fat or too bald to be presented without artifice.

This is not to say, by any means, that all of the male stars were short, obese and ageing; but where such deviations from heroic stature did occur, they were meticulously camouflaged. While film stars were on the whole larger and more dashing than, say, their producers, quite a number of them would not have been qualified to find alternative employment in the police force! Perhaps it is only male chauvinism that insists on screen heroes being at least as tall as their heroines. Sometimes, though, total honesty about relative heights would have given the West a decidedly comic appearance – a touch of James Thurber humour. On such occasions, a box for the gentleman or a ditch for the lady has proved efficacious, as in, say, *Saskatchewan* or *The Sheriff of Fractured Jaw*. But such solutions work only in the closer shots, and it is not always possible to place the hero discreetly uphill from the heroine in the long shots, where the truth may unfortunately become apparent.

Plenty of other examples may be noticed by a sharp-eyed spectator, such as evidence of male corsetry under well-tailored shirts, and even well matched toupées. However, Hollywood's wig-makers are

(Previous page) Arthur Kennedy.

41

Shelley Winters and Alan Ladd in *Saskatchewan* **(1954).**

Jayne Mansfield and Kenneth More in *The Sheriff Of Fractured Jaw* **(1958).**

complete masters of their craft, and most of their customers are careful never to provide evidence of their work by appearing hairless in public. Frank Sinatra's toupée, for example, has only been discussed in print in the context of the bad publicity that he has latterly attracted. Of the major stars, only Sean Connery has dared to make light of his toupée by wearing it for James Bond parts and discarding it for other roles.

The sacrifice is not just a matter of artifice. One report on the making of *The War Wagon* made much play of the good physical shape John Wayne was in at the age of sixty, and after a lung cancer operation – he could still mount his horse nimbly unaided, while Kirk Douglas, a mere stripling of fifty-one, required a carefully placed springboard for the purpose. As, over the years, the really big stars have got old without being superseded, the action cinema has justified their roles by evolving its own picture of age – as a state of seasoned maturity bringing the bounties of experience without any apparent waning of physical powers.

One of the wish-fulfilment gambits that recurs most frequently in the idol-building world of the cinema is the myth of the invincible hero. A very good case could be made out for viewing the cinema (and television) as today's medium for the legends of folklore – particularly in adventure movies, where the heroes may be palpably real yet invested with powers that extend beyond the exceptional towards the superhuman.

Sometimes efforts in this area break down in poor staging or obtrusive use of doubles and other substitutes – remember Victor Mature's life and death struggle with a stuffed lion in the 1949 *Samson and Delilah*? Extraordinary effects, though, can be achieved by using the cinema's resources to extend the agility of stars who are already natural athletes. In his book-length interview with Peter Bogdanovich, Alan Dwan has revealed some of the secrets behind the Douglas Fairbanks *Robin Hood* (1922), which he directed:

'Somebody proposed the story to Doug, and he wasn't interested.

' "I don't want to play a flat-footed Englishman walking through the woods," is the way he put it . . .'

[Later, after the sets were completed . . .]

'When Doug came back from New York, he saw these sets and ran right out of the studio. "I can't compete with those," he said. "That's not me. What can I do in those big sets?" And he was ready to call it off.

'Well, there was a big balcony up high, and on its rail I hung a great big magnificent sweeping drape, made of burlap, but hand-painted to look like a piece of tapestry. I got Doug back to the studio and I said, "Now, look, Doug, you get into a fight down here with some of these knights that are after you, and you fight your way all the way up those stairs round that curve, and finally you get up onto the balcony. Men come out the other door and now you're stuck in the middle, fighting knights over here and knights over there." I paused a minute. He said, "Then?" I said, "Then you jump up on the rail." And I did it for him – so now I'm 50 feet off the stone floor. "You're fighting them on the rail, but they're too much for

SPOT THE TALL GUYS!
Mickey Rooney in *The Last Mile*.
Humphrey Bogart and James
Cagney in *The Oklahoma Kid*.
Edward G. Robinson in *Little Caesar*.
James Stewart with Marlene
Dietrich in *Destry Rides Again*.
Lee Marvin and Paul Newman in
Pocket Money.
Audie Murphy in *To Hell And Back*.
Alan Ladd.
Gary Cooper in *The Real Glory*.

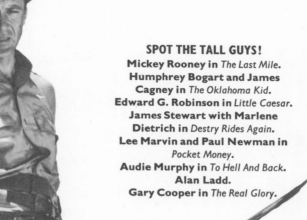

43

Victor Mature wrestling with a lion in Cecil B. deMille's *Samson And Delilah* **(1949).**

you – they're crowding you." He said, "So?" I said, "So you *jump* into the curtain," and I jumped into the curtain – under which I had put a scoop that kids use to slide down – and I went swoosh to the ground, struck one of his poses, and said, "You run out here under the arch and get away." Well, he went up and jumped in the curtain, came down, and then got everybody he knew to come over and see him do the trick! Then he looked up at those high windows, and I told him, "You suddenly appear in that window up there." He said, "How the hell do I get in that window? A fireman couldn't get me up there." I said, "Why, outside – you go up the wall by climbing the vines." "How do I get onto the vines – swim the moat in my armour, or what?" I said, "no". There was a little wall down in the foreground and I had a trampoline on the end of it. "You hit the trampoline and it will throw you into the vines." So he tried it, and boom! – again everybody had to come in and see him do that. Up he crawled and appeared in the window, and that was it – he was sold – we were into *Robin Hood*. Now he was no longer the flat-footed Englishman walking through the woods – he was agile, a bird in flight . . .'

Even when the invincible hero cannot offer quite the sheer physical exhilaration of a Fairbanks, he is still a reassuring spectacle. The legend of invincibility is particularly comforting in the cinema, because of the natural degree of empathy between audience and character; it is not surprising that it has appeared in so many cinematic guises. Before Fairbanks, the Italian spectaculars had

Douglas Fairbanks in exuberant form in *The Three Musketeers* **(1921).**

Kirk Douglas and John Wayne in *The War Wagon* **(1967).**

44

'Maciste', an archetypal strongman who started as a character in *Cabiria* (1914) and reappeared in his own series, with the actor taking the name of the character and continuing in business until 1928. The Maciste character was revived in the second coming of the Italian spectacular, which broke into the international field in 1957 (it had never stopped as a product for domestic consumption) with Steve Reeves, Mr America of 1947 and later Mr World and Mr Universe, playing *Hercules*. The trouble with the revived genre was simple lack of interest, except when it managed to break away from the straight muscleman formula. Nevertheless, the taste of Italian audiences for repetition of a formula is such that countless movies were made with the interchangeable Hercules, Goliath, Maciste and Ursus figures performing low-budget prodigies of strength. The whole Italian spectacular scene fizzled out later in bizarre attempts to diversify – with oriental settings, swashbucklers, and even Scottish spectaculars with a clan called *I Macgregors* as well as curious hybrids in which centurians were pitted against samurai.

The primitive western was another playground of invincibility. Nowhere was the cinema's childhood kept going longer than in the cheapie westerns which right up to the 50s maintained a naïveté that even television series could not get away with today. The straight-forward conflict of good guys and bad guys, an essential part of most people's idea of the western, was very much the prerogative of the B-feature – the business of Buck Jones and Ken Maynard, or at a less primitive level Randolph Scott and Joel McCrea. Once the

MUSCLEMEN IN ITALY:
Maciste in *Cabiria* (1914), and Steve Reeves in *Hercules Unchained*.

45

western emerged into the more self-conscious domain of the A-feature, issues more complex than good versus bad intruded, or sometimes the very simplicity of the conflict was used to give the proceedings the heightened quality of a ritual.

It was in Italy that the invincible western hero was reborn, shorn of the complications and ambiguities of the more ambitious postwar Hollywood westerns. One of the replacements for the spectacular as a staple product of the Italian cinema was the 'spaghetti western'. The Man-With-No-Name character played by Clint Eastwood stemmed from a very European conception of the mythological qualities of the western. Sergio Leone, the director of *For a Fistful of Dollars* and its successors, was clearly hooked on the ritual qualities of the western, which he stressed by formalizing the gun-play to the extent of making it totally ludicrous as action. The same tendency can be seen in his handling of the central character. A very restricted view of the traditional western hero – the coolness, the infallibility, the speed with a gun – has been taken to an almost psychopathic extreme. Charles Bronson, as *l'uomo dell 'armonica* in Leone's *Once Upon A Time In the West*, recently gave us an almost archetypal version of this psychopathic hero, haunting his long-pursued enemy like a vengeful ghost, an instrument of fate, and answering his 'Who are you?' with a list of names of dead men.

Leone's other source may have been samurai movies, particularly those of Akira Kurosawa such as *The Seven Samurai* and *Yojimbo*. This

B-FEATURE WESTERN HEROES
Gene Autry in *The Old West*. Roy Rogers and Trigger. William Boyd in *The Frontiersman*. Ken Maynard in *The Trail Drive*.

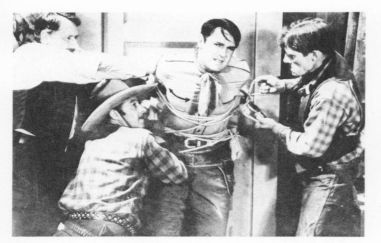

46

again takes us back to the western, through Kurosawa's stated admiration of John Ford, but it also explains the amount of posturing that accompanies Leone's gun-play – the convention of sword fights in samurai movies is that they start with almost static squaring-up, and tentative side-ways movements. There is a strong link between the western and the samurai movie, though this does not mean that their conventions are interchangeable: the characterization of an elite aristocracy of professional killer-heroes, the romantic stylization of personal combat and the introduction of laconic witty dialogue in *The Magnificent Seven* were all derived from the original *Seven Samurai* and in their turn influenced later spy movies, westerns and other hero-centred genres.

By the 60s, the samurai movie, the indigenous popular adventure form, again typified by an invincible hero, became one of the dominant forms on Japanese television. Films involving samurai had been around for a long time before the enormous success of *The Seven Samurai* brought them to international notice (just as Italian spectaculars continued to be made pretty continuously for home consumption between their early successes before 1920 and their post-Hercules boom in the late 50s). But many of the earlier films with samurai were very far from being adventure movies, for instance Kenji Mizoguchi's *The Loyal Forty-Seven Ronin of the Genroku Era* (1942), which lasts around four hours and ends with a prolonged scene in which (mainly off screen) all forty-seven, plus one girl, commit hara kiri in succession.

THE A-FEATURE WESTERN
John Ford's *Cheyenne Autumn.*
Robert Aldrich's *The Last Sunset.*
Robert Mitchum, Teresa Wright and
Judith Anderson in Raoul Walsh's
Pursued. **Gary Cooper in Fred**
Zinnemann's *High Noon.*

The Chinese equivalent of the samurai movie is the Kung-Fu epic, as produced in large quantities by the Shaw Brothers, Run Run and Run Me, in Hong Kong. They have been in business since the late 40s, finding their audiences also on Formosa and among expatriate Chinese populations in Singapore, Hawaii and on the American West Coast. Some of their earlier work had ambitions in the quality market: Run Run Shaw co-produced one of Mizoguchi's master-pieces, *Yang Kwei Fei* (1955), and another of their movies, *The Magnificent Concubine* was shown officially at a Cannes film festival in the mid 60s. Their great successes, though, have been with Kung-Fu, which is an art of what is euphemistically known as self-defence, and the basis of both judo and karate. The Kung-Fu boom outside the Orient started with the showing of a television series, *Kung-Fu*, in the United States, and the acquisition of distribution rights by Warner Brothers in an effort variously known as *Five Fingers of Death*, *Invincible Boxer* or *King Boxer*. This seems likely to be to Kung-Fu movies what *Hercules* was to the Italian spectacular, the film which raises quite unrealistic hopes for a genre really only calculated for home consumption.

In fact, *King Boxer* operates on much the same simple-minded level as a muscleman movie, though instead of feats of strength with expanded polystyrene rocks, it offers extraordinary agility of a kind which even the dumbest spectator can surmise to be produced with trampolines – when a boxer is leaping in the air to kick his opponent in the face, the piece of floor from which he has launched

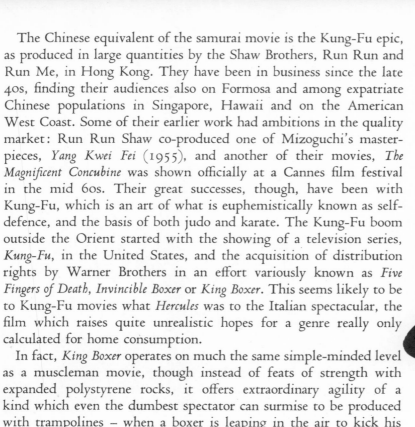

Clint Eastwood, the Man-With-No-Name, in *For A Fistful Of Dollars* **(1964).**

48

King Boxer **in action.**

Steve Reeves, *Hercules Unchained.*

Clint Eastwood.

FOLLOWERS OF JAMES BOND:
James Coburn, *In Like Flint* **(1967).**
Dean Martin, Arthur O'Connell and
Stella Stevens in the first *Matt Helm*
film.

Seven Samurai **(1954). A spellbinding
piece of oriental savagery on which**
The Magnificent Seven **(1961) was based.
Sean Connery and Jill St John**
Diamonds Are Forever **(1971).**

himself is invariably concealed from view. In the very first scene, an old man is set upon by a band of armed thugs, and escapes with only a single minor cut by leaping up out of harm's way on to handy walls and rooftops. The central conflict is between two boxing schools, one good and one so wicked that it even imports Japanese heavies to wipe out the nice guys before the great contest in which they hope to gain power by producing a champion. At the good school, an ex-pupil of the nimble old gent, who turns out to be a veteran boxing teacher, is taught the master's secret iron fist technique, which is entirely lethal. Training for this appears to involve plunging the hands into hot gravel; its use is preceded by red light on the fist and shrieking music like that of the titles sequence in *Ironside* (the music score is almost entirely western in style).

King Boxer has been advertised as the first eastern western, and is not ashamed to borrow a trick or two from Hollywood. One of the few personality traits exhibited by the hero is stoicism: sent by a teacher to get wine from the Chinese version of a saloon, which even has a long bar, he keeps his inscrutable cool while sorely provoked by the heavies. Apart from novelty, the only other treat that the film has to offer non-oriental audiences is the violence (which ties in with a general escalation in cinematic violence that one might suggest comes as an effect rather than a cause of violence in the world at large). Kicking in the face – often in slow motion – is only the start of a catalogue of goodies including the hero's hands being beaten to pulp with clubs. There is also a subjective shot from the view-

James Bond – Sean Connery and Ursula Andress in *Dr No* (1962), the first Bond film.

point of a prostrate fighter, looking up as a nasty person leaps on him with two fingers extended. At this point, British audiences appear to have been deprived of a close shot, for the conventions of the piece would lead one to expect more emphasis to be given to the eyeballs which are lying on the floor in the subsequent long shot. When the hero really gets his iron fist going in the last reel, he is able to grab the remaining heavy's sword by the blade before finally pulverizing him. The first fist blow slows the man up even though the impact has been broken by a wooden pillar. The second time, he is iron fisted into a wall, removing a large patch of stucco. The third, and lethal, blow propels him against the same wall, this time leaving a sizeable dent in the brickwork. The hero, Chao Chih-hao, heaves a sigh of relief and walks away with his faithful Sung Ying Ying. Cut to end title superimposed on sunset. On the strength of *King Boxer*, the prospects of Kung-Fu movies outside their ethnic market seem decidedly short-term. However, at the time of writing, we have yet to see the products of the rival company to the Shaw Brothers, which has as its main asset the big star of the Kung-Fu business, Bruce Lee.

The various forms of invincible hero movie I have mentioned so far are all period pieces. Their modern counterparts are the spy movies, the Bond series and its imitators, some of which kept the Italian studios busy between the spectaculars and the westerns. These entirely mechanical products include a hero called James Tont, who appeared in a number of movies, and even a character called Gold-balls. Spy movies, though, fall somewhat outside the category of machine-age folk art: they are characterized by their knowingly jokey air, and by a lack of moral constraint on the hero which can work as wish-fulfilment in the light-hearted versions, the Matt Helms and Flints, but also decreases the difference between heroes and adversaries – a point that counted for much in the attempts to make serious, downbeat spy movies.

CHAPTER 5
SUSPENSE AND ACTION

There is a view, particularly prevalent in France, that the cinema is not a show or spectacle but a form of writing. However, the potentialities of film are so wide as to make any such restricting definition untenable – cinema can be more-or-less whatever you want to make it. In any case, it has a history largely constructed of shows or spectacles; film as literature in another medium has produced some remarkable works, but they largely belong to the intellectual end of the scale, which did not become dominant until after 1960. By then, the cinema as a mass medium was definitely in decline. But ever since film narrative progressed beyond the Méliès stage of tableaux, the popular cinema has thought in terms of action.

Movie audiences can expect to derive all sorts of satisfaction from the events put before them, and the satisfaction is heightened by identification with the characters on the screen. The most basic of these satisfactions is the happy ending, the fulfilment of our hopes for the people whose lives we have been sharing. One frequent theme of critical carping over the years has been Hollywood's predilection for adding gratuitous happy endings to everything. It is, however, rather less pernicious than a more recent tendency in the search for something called maturity to add equally gratuitous unhappy endings. Even though it had a crassly symbolic purpose, the demise of Jason Robards, the splendid hero of Sam Peckinpah's *The Ballad of Cable Hogue* belongs in this category – having made his fortune by finding water beside a trail through the desert, he is accidentally run down by a motor car, the very device that has convinced him that the time has come to sell out and retire from the water business.

Jason Robards and Stella Stevens in *The Ballad Of Cable Hogue.*

I remember the late Anthony Mann saying that there was nothing people liked to see as much as characters succeeding in what they set out to do, a thesis which he flippantly extended to include Hamlet – after all the guy set out to kill his uncle. The western, of which Mann was one of the finest exponents, is only one of the genres of which the success story is characteristic. Where John Ford's films often centre on glory in defeat, Mann's westerns are about the cost of succeeding: in *Bend of the River* and *The Man from Laramie*, James Stewart respectively gets the supplies to the settlers and finds out who gave guns to the Indians who massacred a cavalry

patrol including his kid brother, but in both cases succeeds only at the expense of physical maltreatment and the death of Arthur Kennedy (who may emerge as the heavy in both cases but initially appears among the most likeable characters in the two films). In *Man of the West*, Gary Cooper retrieves the money with which he has been entrusted, and is able to return home, but only after killing most of his relatives. The great Anthony Mann success story, though, is the one which prompted his remark in the first place, *El Cid*, in which Charlton Heston manages to put the Moors to flight even after his death – as he expires, he orders that his body should be strapped on his horse to ride out at the head of his troops.

Beyond the obvious satisfaction of the happy ending, the movies

Anthony Mann's Westerns
Bend Of The River **(1951).**
The Man From Laramie **(1955).**
Arthur Kennedy about to be lynched
in *Bend Of The River.*

James Stewart and Arthur Kennedy
in *The Man From Laramie*.

James Stewart as
The Man From Laramie.

genuinely offer something for everyone. For those who feel there might be kicks in slapping girls around there are spy movies; perfect elegance, agility and grace can be found in Fred Astaire movies; there is even something for the masochists in many a Kirk Douglas movie. Satisfaction through identification is only one of the rewards available to the film audience – there may be other delights, either intellectual or sensual. No aspect of the cinema has been more generally neglected than its sensual qualities, possibly because they are almost impossible to deal with adequately in words. To do so at any length here would involve waxing lyrical about the musical, for sensuality in the cinema is less concerned with photographic exquisiteness than with movement. It is worth noting, though, that adventure movies can also work very powerfully on a sensual level of sheer physical exhilaration. Sometimes the movies may be relatively undistinguished: for instance, the title sequences of *The War Wagon* and *Something Big* both use the combination of a strongly rythmic number with a lot of movement, which may be a cliché of latter-day Hollywood but can still produce a remarkably stirring effect. Integrated into the dramatic structure of a really fine film, exploitation of sensual excitement has produced some of the cinema's really unforgettable moments – one of these for me is the arrival of the U.S. Cavalry at the confrontation between Lionel Barrymore's men and those of the railroad in King Vidor's *Duel in the Sun*.

Gary Cooper in *Man Of The West* **(1958).**

But the most usual companion of action in the movies is suspense, which is to be found in a far wider range of films than those characterized as thrillers. Suspense, after all, is a matter of involving the feelings of the spectator in the outcome of the action. Most storytelling contains an element of suspense, though the immediacy of the movies makes it more important than it generally is in other media. The thriller is merely a generic term for narratives in which suspense plays a dominant role.

Suspense will emerge from delay in fulfilling the spectator's desires or expectations or in resolving his fears. There are very few film genres from which it is largely absent. The musical, which offers most of its rewards on a non-narrative level, is one. Hard-core pornography, at its current stage of development, is another: by giving their all with the greatest alacrity, hard-core offerings are left with nothing beyond repetition with variations. Lacking the requisite notions of dramatic construction, they quite literally grind themselves into the ground.

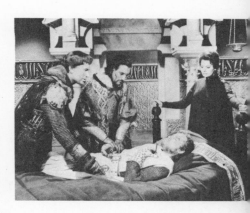

The great Anthony Mann success story, *El Cid* **(1961), starring Charlton Heston.**

The most primitive cinematic structure built around suspense is the action climax in which, for example, the heroine is in the power of the heavies while the hero dashes to the rescue, and the question is, will he get there in time? Well, of course, he will and so will his equivalents in other situations: the settlers holding out against the Indians, the ammunition getting down to the crucial level of one bullet per female head to forestall a fate worse than death at the hands of the lecherous savages (we are, you will realize, dealing with the products of 1910 or thereabouts), but the U.S. Cavalry, led by a wholesome young officer who is probably courting the

SOMETHING FOR EVERYONE
Kicks from sadism. Perfect elegance,
Fred Astaire and Ginger Rogers.
Masochism, Kirk Douglas in
Man Without A Star **(1955).**

The War Wagon (1967).

settler's daughter, is on the way. It does not take a very sophisticated audience to realize that such dramas have only one likely outcome, ending in triumph of the good guys – this was a firmly established rule well before the arrival of the Production Code made comeuppance for all malefactors an absolute dogma.

Knowing the outcome does not make the audience immune from even the simplest forms of suspense, but acclimatization to the inevitability of the happy ending is likely to reduce the tension that gets across. Still, there is always the chance that the unexpected could happen – in Alfred Hitchcock's *Sabotage*, a suspense sequence built around a small boy unwittingly carrying a time bomb on a bus, ends in an explosion. I believe that Hitchcock sees this as a mistake, but in the context of thrillers as a whole rather than of the particular film, its effect is salutary, a reminder that the reassuring rules do not always work.

Within the final reel climax where the rules can be expected to apply, there are various devices that will heighten the tension. The classical device for achieving a thrilling climax is intercutting: shots of the heroine menaced by the heavy alternated with others of the hero galloping to the rescue. Unless the film has been sufficiently powerful to make us feel really strongly for the characters, this is likely to be a big yawn. A bit of physical excitement can help here – tracking shots, the camera travelling rapidly in front of the hero's horse as he comes to the rescue, as it did with the noble Ku Klux Klansmen in D. W. Griffith's *The Birth of a Nation* coming to save the Little Colonel's sweetheart from the depredations of the ferocious blacks (who had been happy darkies until they were led astray by greedy carpetbaggers and lascivious mulattoes). The tracking movement accentuates the degree of frenzy in the climax and the physical impression of the distance that the hero is having to cover in order to arrive in the nick of time. A related device is used in the one effective shot in J. Lee Thompson's *North West Frontier* – the train in which Kenneth Moore, Lauren Bacall and their companions are escaping is pursued by tribesmen on horseback; the train is chuffing furiously down the track with riders nearly catching up on both sides as the camera, in what seems a remarkable piece of timing, whizzes across the track in the path of the oncoming train and pursuers. The camera movement at right angles to that of the chase that is coming towards us in the image gives a quite unexpected impetus to the action.

In our basic action climax situation, with the hero galloping to the rescue, the physical heightening of the tracking shot will only help a bit in moving audiences towards the edges of their seats. So there are prolonging devices – frustration: a false trail or some impassable obstacle, a river that is too fast or deep to ford, a ravine too steep to cross; the rescuer has to go back and try a different approach. Perhaps an alternative set of adversaries gets in the way – if outlaws have the heroine in their power, then there might be a band of war-painted Comanches on the loose having to be avoided or confronted. Or some injury to man or horse might slow them down. All these things serve to delay the moment when salvation

SUSPENSE
Will the heroine be rescued in
time???

Hitchcock's *Sabotage* **(1942).**

Northwest Frontier.

D. W. Griffith's Civil War epic,
The Birth Of A Nation **(1914).**

finally arrives; suspense is as much as anything a matter of slowing down, delaying, drawing out the action.

Meanwhile the heroine is in terrible trouble, which can also be milked for suspense. Within the limits of the censorship prevalent at the time, the heavy can be allowed to make a start with his dastardly designs; at the very least, he should finally have the innocent maiden in his clutches when her rescuer arrives. Before this moment comes, ways will have been found of prolonging the agony (which is evidently necessary to balance the time taken by the hero's problems, if he is not to find his loved one has been thoroughly violated while he has been overcoming the various reverses that have been thrown in his way). Our heroine may be an innocent flower but she is also able bodied and well endowed with moral fibre; she is not just going to resign herself to her fate. She is likely to make every attempt to stop the heavy, putting locked doors between herself and him, and when these are of no avail, dodging behind any item of furniture that will shield her and hurling any missiles that come to hand. She might even get hold of a knife, which will be wrested from her grip just before the nick of time which produces the hero. All her attempts at resistance provide the villain with opportunities to demonstrate his power by smashing down doors and throwing aside tables. Apart from suggesting that he is such a formidable adversary that the outcome of the final struggle with the hero is not quite as certain as it ought to be, the inexorable progress of the heavy makes it quite clear that if the hero fails to show, there is no possible doubt that the heroine has had it (whatever 'it' may be). Anyway, in our hypothetical period piece, the heroine is really helpless because she is that now forgotten creature, just a woman. The spectacle of vulnerable innocence and evil strength may help involve the audience in the suspense even though the outcome is predetermined; alternatively, there are two identification figures of aspiring rapist and potential victim to exercise some of the spectators' fantasies.

One recipe for heightening suspense which appeared quite early in the development of the movies, and certainly in time for our action-packed two-reeler, is the addition of a strong element of physical danger. There is not very much that you can do with the heroine beyond changing the nature of the threat to her by tying her to the railroad track when the express is on its way. This solves the problem of what to do with her while the hero and the villain are fighting it out. The struggle is no longer the centre of the suspense except in that the speed with which it is concluded is germane to the central question of whether the heroine can be untied before she is trisected by the train.

Although the heroine tied to the rails is one of the more famous images in the cinema, danger can be used to much greater effect in other ways. A recent *McLeod* segment in the *Saturday Mystery Movie* television series had a riveting moment when Dennis Weaver grabbed hold of the helicopter in which the heavies were escaping from a New York rooftop; a vertiginous shot looks down on him as the helicopter sweeps away from the roof and the streets open out

Killer's Kiss.
Piccadilly Third Stop.
Edge Of Eternity.

ALFRED HITCHCOCK
Doris Day as the mother of the
kidnapped boy in
The Man Who Knew Too Much **(1956).**

way below. Even on television, this provides a sharp jolt to the viewer. In Don Siegel's *Edge of Eternity*, it does not matter to us that we know the ending when Mickey Shaughnessy and Cornel Wilde slug it out as they sway precariously on a container of a cable transporter over the Grand Canyon. Vertigo is not the only sort of audience fear which can be summoned up to help the suspense. In a minor British movie, *Piccadilly Third Stop*, there is a fight on the track of the London Underground, which provides the unsettling spectacle of heads being pushed down towards the live rail. The choice of weapons can also increase our unease: in Stanley Kubrick's early film *Killer's Kiss*, there is a fight in a warehouse which is used to store shop-window mannequins and their spare parts. The weapons are snatched from the fire-fighting kit: felling axe versus crowbar. The effect of the axe, which is being wielded by the sadistic heavy (Frank Silvera), is demonstrated by its effects on the mannequins, which fall maimed at every blow.

At least for the past quarter of a century, the maker of thrillers has been faced with a knowing audience which is not going to be much thrilled by the basic suspense gambits. Some way has to be devised of breaking through our veneer of sophistication, of undermining our confidence before we will surrender to the film's suspense. Scaring us with spectacular danger is one method, though of limited application. It works splendidly in one of the fights in *How the West Was Won* which is staged among huge logs that have become unhitched and are rolling around on an open freight car in a train which is travelling over a bendy, mountainous track.

However, it is rarely possible to conduct a whole film on purely physical thrills. The most reliable basis for suspense is emotional involvement with the characters. They, after all, do not know that they are in a world governed by the Production Code, and we may temporarily forget that all is going to be well in the end if our feelings are tied up in sharing their predicament. Take away the assurance of a happy ending by putting the hero on the wrong side of the law (Sterling Hayden in Stanley Kubrick's *The Killing*), or in an ambiguous position (Marlon Brando in Elia Kazan's *On the Waterfront*), and we have cause for apprehension. This additional source of suspense relies on the audience having seen enough movies to know the rules. The most inspired use of this knowledge was made in *Psycho*, where Hitchcock took everyone aback by doing the one thing which is really never done – killing off his biggest star a third of the way through the picture. But then, even those who maintain that they did not have the pants scared off them by their first viewing of *Psycho* agree that Hitchcock is unrivalled as a generator of suspense, whatever else he may or may not be intending to do.

With Hitchcock, more than with anyone else, suspense is bound up with identification – he works with a very clear knowledge of the effect that every detail of his films will have on their audiences. He knows, too, that suspense cannot be produced instantly; it has to be built up carefully. One of the techniques which he uses with great cunning is building the suspense in blocks which are obliquely

Misfortunes for Cary Grant in *North By North West* **(1959).**

The Wrong Man **(1957), Henry Fonda with Vera Miles.**

related to the final, predetermined outcome. There is not going to be much doubt in our mind that Farley Granger will manage to clear himself of the murder committed by Robert Walker in *Strangers on a Train*, and none at all that Doris Day and James Stewart will get their kidnapped son back unharmed in the second, and better, version of *The Man Who Knew Too Much*. So the suspense is built less on the ultimate outcome than on such closer targets as whether Walker will manage to reach the crucial cigarette lighter which he has accidentally dropped down a drain, or whether the sedatives that Stewart has given Doris Day will have begun to work before she realizes that her son has definitely been kidnapped. This latter sequence is crucial to the destruction of audience detachment as it involves us in Doris Day's breakdown. We are unlikely to be able to remain so confidently outside the action after we have witnessed her distressing reduction in a few hours – or some minutes' screen time – from a happy wife, talking about having another child, to the hysterical woman who has to be held down by her husband.

This sequence illustrates an alternative form of suspense, which Hitchcock has made his own. So far, we have largely looked at suspense that is building towards something which we want to happen. Here we have the reverse: suspense building towards something which we hope will not happen. Hitchcock often uses this to cement our complicity with the characters: with Tippi Hedren in *Marnie*, which contains the brilliant sequence in which she has stayed behind after work in order to steal from Sean Connery's safe. She hides in the toilets until her colleagues have departed and then moves silently into action in her stockinged feet. Her shoes are in her coat pockets. While she is stealing from the safe, a cleaner arrives and sets to work on the outside office. One of Marnie's shoes is slipping out of her pocket. Will it fall and alert the cleaner? In the event, it does fall, but does not disturb the cleaner, who is deaf. What the business with the shoe has done is to move our reaction from one of detached interest to complicity in the theft – we are strongly hoping that the shoe will not fall.

Hitchcock is generally accepted as the greatest suspense director. But his suspense is linked to themes which make him anything but an adventure film director. Indeed, he appears totally opposed to adventure, the ultimate devotee of the quiet life. For his characters who by accident or desire are lifted out of their familiar routine, the experience is likely to be a nightmare, even if it is presented with considerable humour, like Cary Grant's misfortunes in *North by Northwest*. But the couple in both versions of *The Man Who Knew Too Much* have their child kidnapped, Henry Fonda in *The Wrong Man* is convicted of a murder which he did not commit, and Janet Leigh is butchered in the shower in *Psycho*. She at least had a choice, and however unsatisfactory her lot may have been, she would clearly have been well advised to accept it. Without attributing any metaphysical dimension to the evil that is abroad in Hitchcock's world, we can recognize the perils that await anyone unwise enough or unlucky enough to venture into the unknown.

The escape from burning Atlanta in
Gone With The Wind **(1939).**

CHAPTER 6
ADVENTURE IN HISTORY

Todd Armstrong in
Jason And The Argonauts **(1963), directed
by Don Chaffey.**

It would not be very illuminating to attempt an overall history of adventure in the cinema. As we have already seen, there is no identifiable genre which can be labelled as The Adventure Movie. Adventure is distributed in varying proportions through most of the cinema, popping up conspicuously in such distinct forms as the weepie – historical romances, in particular, often contain a generous measure of swashbuckling adventure. The few tolerable moments in *Gone With the Wind* are action scenes like the escape from burning Atlanta, perhaps because they offer brief respites from Vivien Leigh doing her Southern belle number.

Although the range of adventure movies is wide, some generalizations can be made. Unlike the films of Alfred Hitchcock, the adventure movie has a feeling towards action, excitement and danger that is clearly positive, however much this may be qualified by showing us the less likeable aspects of the hero's character or actions. The end of the film may show the hero growing up, settling down and joining the Establishment, but (as the righteous endings imposed by the Production Code on crime movies frequently demonstrated) a quick change of direction in the last reel is rarely enough to alter the feeling of the picture, and the audience will be left remembering the adventure as more desirable than the settling down. The positive feeling for adventure will emerge both from the exhilaration of the action itself and from the provision of identification figures among the leading characters. The other common factor among adventure movies is a negative one, setting: the one unlikely location for adventure is here and now. Perhaps to give the action an aura of exoticism and romance, perhaps to reassure the audience that the enviable adventures will remain enviably out of reach, the accepted setting is another time and, for most audiences, another place.

Movies set in the historical past have been turned out steadily, covering the whole range from ancient civilizations up to, say, World War I, but they have always been much in the minority. Except for the brief heyday of the Italian spectacular and the longer-term success of the western, they have never built up the complex iconography developed in a genre like the crime picture. They have in common mainly a set of very rudimentary historical preconceptions – the good examples stand on their own, rather than belonging also in the context of a developing genre.

In its dealings with ancient civilizations, the cinema has largely fought shy of their mythology and preferred to look for inspiration in their history. Among the exceptions is, surprisingly, a British movie, Don Chaffey's lively *Jason and the Argonauts*. Although this is let down by its visualization of Olympus, with the immortals using the swimming pool like a gigantic television set for looking in on human intrigues, it has seized on mythology as a new format for the monster movie. The special effects – from iron man to an army of skeletons – are nicely conceived, but sometimes shakily realized, suffering from blue edges and visible strings. Chaffey was also responsible for one of the cinema's few excursions into the prehistoric, the second version (by Hammer) of *One Million Years B.C.*,

One Million Years B.C. **(1966) also directed by Don Chaffey, starred Raquel Welch and some engaging prehistoric monsters.**

71

Gold For The Caesars **(1962).**

Reg Park in Vittorio Cottafavi's
Hercules Conquers Atlantis **(1961).**

which has rather less going for it than *Jason and the Argonauts* because of the boredom inherent in having characters who can converse only in grunts. But there are again some engaging monsters, including a predatory pterodactyl which abducts the heroine, Raquel Welch, who is mostly occupied in demonstrating how the resourceful primitive girl could turn animal skins into impeccably cut mini-dresses. Beyond the monster appeal and the pin-up values, the film is memorable only for its cavalier way with palaeontology, giving us together in one film the best of many million years of evolution.

Italian spectaculars flirted with mythology as the best context for exercising their muscle-men, but the outcome was rarely worth watching. I can think of no other area of big business film-making which worked to such low standards. Budgets, which were sometimes stretched so tightly that even badly fogged footage was used to save retakes, rarely ran to the hire of directors with any talent. Some of the better-funded efforts were made with directors from abroad, but of the native directors, only two managed any number of good spectaculars. One was Riccardo Freda, who had been making them since the 40s, and also directed the action sequences for a couple of spectaculars by André de Toth, *The Mongols* (1961) and *Gold for the Caesars* (1962). The other was Vittorio Cottafavi, who made the best of all the mythological films, and probably the best Italian spectacular, *Hercules Conquers Atlantis*. This must have been almost unique in being made with an adequate (and shrewdly spent) budget, and in being shot in 70mm Super Technirama. Where financial limitations might have defeated him, in staging the destruction of Atlantis, Cottafavi made use of Haroun Tazieff's documentary footage of volcanic eruptions to suggest a cataclysmic upheaval.

Cottafavi's Hercules is a more inventively handled character than his namesakes in other films (in the world of the Italian spectacular, Hercules is not the particular guy who did the Five Labours, but a general name for almost any well-disposed strong man). Instead of the lugubrious and utterly mechanical figure always ready to flex an over-developed muscle in a good cause, Cottafavi's Hercules (Reg Park) is lazy, good natured, and reluctant to fight – it takes drugged wine to keep him on the expedition ship to Atlantis which has been threatening Greece.

Atlantis, under its ferocious queen, Antinea, is able to call on dark and magical forces drawn from the past and from Uranus, the god who had been defeated by Zeus. Antinea is bent on conquest and is training up a military élite of blond supermen – one of the themes of the film is an extended parallel with Nazism. There is a strong suggestion of the concentration camp in the prison pit which contains those who will not or cannot conform to the queen's Aryan ideal.

But the thematic content of the film is not pressed at the expense of the entertainment expected in a spectacular. Hercules still performs his prodigious feats in contriving that the rays of the sun can fall on and destroy the rock which is the source of the magical powers; the destruction of the rock brings with it the destruction

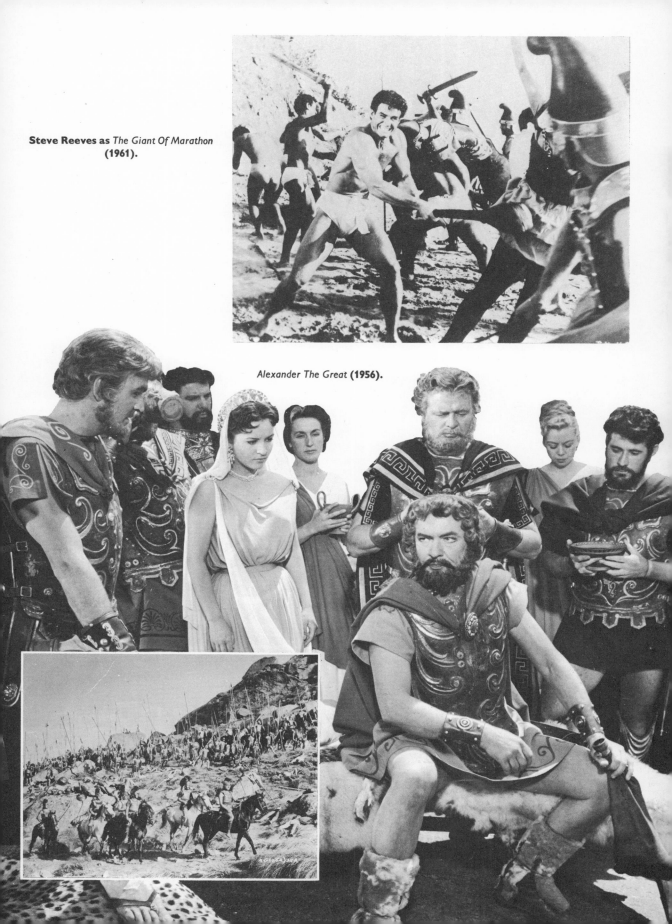

Steve Reeves as *The Giant Of Marathon* **(1961).**

Alexander The Great **(1956).**

**Howard Hawks' view of the building
of the pyramids in**
Land Of The Pharaohs.

300 Spartans **(1962) directed by
Rudolph Maté.**

of Atlantis. In the disparity between the action of one man and the magnitude of its results, we may find another parallel, this time with the hydrogen bomb. Again, the parallel is there to be found rather than pushed at the paying customers, who will not have come for intellectual stimulation. Cottafavi, an extremely intelligent man whose first films were part of the Italian neo-realist movement, and who has directed work by Sophocles, Molière, Dostoyevsky, Lorca and Pirandello for Italian television, does not give any evidence of despising the genre. Where a sophisticated director faced with making a muscle-man epic might be expected either to show his contempt for the genre by sending it up or to try redeeming it with a weight of message heavy enough to undermine it as a genre entertainment, Cottafavi takes the genre and works brilliantly within it with a strength and economy in his images that exactly matches the nature of his story as a fable.

Some elements of mythology carry over into films that are, broadly speaking, historical. Steve Reeves lends his muscular invincibility to Jacques Tourneur's *The Giant of Marathon*, a film that also shows considerable skill in getting the most out of a limited number of extras. Where earnest attempts have been made at historical accuracy, the result has an unfortunate tendency, as in Robert Rossen's stolid *Alexander the Great*, to be less convincing than pictures which are historically complete fabrications.

Occasionally a documentary approach does pay. Howard Hawks managed a stunning account of pyramid building in *Land of the Pharaohs*, which had William Faulkner as one of its three script-writers. The trouble came with the people. As Hawks said to Peter Bogdanovich: 'I don't know how a Pharaoh talks. And Faulkner didn't know. None of us knew. We thought it'd be an interesting story, the building of a pyramid, but then we had to have a plot, and we didn't really feel close to any of it. . . . I got a feeling we were doing repetitive scenes and it was awfully hard to deepen them because we didn't know how those Egyptians thought or what they said. All we knew about them was this strange desire to amass a fortune to be used in their second life, as they called it. So you don't know what to try for at all. You don't know whether to make the girl a little more evil or the Pharoah a little more dominating. You kind of lose all sense of values. You don't know who somebody's

for and if you don't have a rooting interest and you're not for somebody, then you haven't got a picture.'

Even so, *Land of the Pharaohs* was very much livelier than most ancient epics, managing even on a personal level to avoid the boredom which is the prevailing fault of the genre. Another piece of non-boring antiquity, this time on a much smaller scale, was Rudolph Maté's picture about Thermopylae, *The 300 Spartans*. Veteran Hollywood action directors seem to be the ones best equipped to deal with spectaculars, perhaps because they have been conditioned to believe that failure to entertain is the greatest failure of all. For example, compare the power of Richard Fleischer's *Barabbas* with the crippling boredom of Alf Sjöberg's earlier

Anthony Quinn in Richard Fleischer's *Barabbas* **(1962).**

Quo Vadis **with Peter Ustinov as Nero and Patricia Laffan as Poppaea providing far more diversion than the Christian Robert Taylor and Deborah Kerr.**

Cleopatra (Elizabeth Taylor) making her first appearance before Caesar (Rex Harrison) in the 1962 version of *Cleopatra* with Richard Burton as Mark Antony.

Swedish version of Per Lagerkvist's novel; for a partial exception, there is Anthony Mann's failure to make anything much out of *The Fall of the Roman Empire*.

Another action director who has managed to make something of an epic is Raoul Walsh with *Esther and the King*, one of the few biblical pictures to be made among the Italian spectaculars (a less successful one, with more pretensions, was Robert Aldrich's *Sodom and Gomorrah*). For the major film companies, the Holy Land is a place fraught with peril. When the level of expenditure demands that you try to please everyone and make certain to offend no-one, religion presents terrible problems: every thought has to be laundered by a panel of advisory clerics; there has to be one of everything, like a bad joke – 'have you heard the one about the Protestant, the Jesuit and the Rabbi'. . . . There is so little that will please them all, and the menu put before the audience is likely to have all the individuality and piquancy of hospital cooking. Verily, piety is the handmaiden of boredom.

As we move from B.C. to A.D., we have the glory and the decadence of Imperial Rome, which might seem like a promising subject for the movies, were it not for the arrival on the scene of spoil-sport Christianity. The would-be commercials for religion from the pens of Lew Wallace, Henryk Sienkiewicz and Lloyd C. Douglas turned into films that were unlikely to produce any converts. From *Ben-Hur* (silent or sound versions), people remember the chariot race. In Mervyn LeRoy's *Quo Vadis*, Peter Ustinov and

Gina Lollobrigida in
Solomon And Sheba.

Patricia Laffan as Nero and Poppaea are considerably more diverting and memorable than Robert Taylor and Deborah Kerr as convert and Christian. From *The Robe*, there is nothing worth remembering except for the novel shape of the screen, Cinemascope's 2.5:1 ratio, just waiting for a director who would know what to do with it.

The ancient spectacular has been, on the whole, a graveyard for ambitions, a genre in which even the most talented directors have finished by achieving only a fraction of what they intended. One might spare a word of praise, though, for Joseph L. Mankiewicz's work on the Burton/Taylor *Cleopatra*, much maligned because of its galloping budget, but actually an honourable and intelligent piece of work, though perhaps a little lacking in the more demonstrative qualities of showmanship. It is also remarkable for the conception of its central character – rather than relying on post-Victorian ideas of regality, it uses Elizabeth Taylor's presence as an actress to embody Cleopatra's power as a queen. Other epics are memorable only for occasional images. King Vidor's *Solomon and Sheba*, nobbled from the start by having Yul Brynner and Gina Lollobrigida walking on in the title roles, is pitiably short on sensuality, with the most half-hearted orgy sequence imaginable, but it does have a battle in which the heavies, dazzled by the reflections in the burnished shields of the outnumbered good guys, all ride off the edge of a ravine. Stanley Kubrick's *Spartacus* has a few moments of visual power like the burning of a tented encampment at night (a triumph of photography by Russel Metty). Douglas Sirk's *Sign of the Pagan* is less notable for Jack Palance going full out to be Attila the Hun than for some dream-like images of dignitaries of the early church moving silently by boat across mist-covered waters.

Curiously enough, with the arrival of the Dark Ages, things begin to look up in the realms of film history. The period between the Fall of Rome and the Renaissance has been conspicuously more rewarding cinematically than the more sophisticated earlier societies. In the movies, it is a period in which the conflicts are of a sort that can be solved by violent action rather than by argument or intrigue.

The Dark Ages in the cinema have to live up to accepted connotations of pillage, murder and rape – within the limits of the family picture, of course. The outstanding success in this is Richard Fleischer's *The Vikings*, which views its subjects' rude vigour with a relish that takes in its stride pecked-out eyes and lopped-off hands. The jovial humour of the script (by Calder Willingham, later co-author of the script for *The Graduate*) is nicely captured in a scene between British princess Morgana (Janet Leigh) and her older and less well endowed companion, who are in the power of the Vikings, held prisoner in a boat moored in the fjord by their stronghold. Both are expecting that violation is on the way, a possibility which is worrying Morgana very much more than her companion.

A less successful attempt at a jolly celebration of Viking energy was Jack Cardiff's *The Long Ships* with Richard Widmark seeming intent on having fun at the film's expense and Sidney Poitier looking very strange in long hair as a Moor. A much more hard-bitten view of the Vikings was offered by an Italian picture *Fury of the Vikings*,

Kirk Douglas as *Spartacus* **(1966).**

Jack Palance as Attila the Hun, in
Sign Of The Pagan (1954).

The Dark Ages on the screen –
Richard Fleischer's *The Vikings* (1957).
Jack Cardiff's *The Long Ships* (1964)
with Sidney Poitier and
Richard Widmark.

starring Cameron Mitchell and directed and photographed by Mario Bava (who had been cinematographer on *Esther and the King* and is said to have directed part of *The Giant of Marathon*). As one might expect from a director who was the leading light in Italian horror movies, this is a notably grim affair, though relieved by some strikingly staged action scenes – in one, possibly more remarkable than convincing, arrows shot into the cracks between the stones of a castle wall are used as footholds for scaling it.

Clive Donner's *Alfred The Great* **(1969)** starred David Hemmings as Alfred.

The Vikings have been sparsely covered by the cinema; its big pre-Renaissance number is British chivalry, from its legendary Arthurian origins to the Wars of the Roses. As in any genre, only a small proportion rise above the norm, which in this case means the monotonous clash of steel alternating with wooden dialogue. Cornel Wilde's *Lancelot and Guinevere*, for instance, is distinguished by Wilde's preoccupation with making the violence as real as possible. This was to be worked out more fully in Wilde's next picture, *The Naked Prey*, which brings a painful degree of realism to the predicament of a solitary man being hunted in the jungle. *Lancelot and Guinevere* recognizes that the long sword was a heavy two-handed weapon suitable for hacking rather than fencing; when it connected, it would do a lot of damage, demonstrated in the film by a blow from Lancelot's sword that cuts through his opponent's shoulder right down to the chest.

An ambitious and unjustly neglected piece of work was Clive Donner's *Alfred the Great*, a big film which, four years after its production, has received only a limited showing. It shows evidence of having had trouble in the cutting rooms, and suffers grievously from the *Land of the Pharaohs* problem of not knowing the way they talked – the dialogue was for most critics an insuperable obstacle to seeing anything in the film. Yet it is interesting even from a thematic angle, one of the few angles from which most reviewers can approach the cinema – it shows how Alfred's conversion to Christianity only increases his involvement in violence. Unlike most spectaculars, which take place under skies of picture postcard blue, it takes advantage of the changeability of the British climate as a dramatic element in the film. It also has some of the best staged and filmed battles I have seen. The problem with battle scenes is showing where everyone is and giving a coherent picture of the progress of the action as a whole. Just how difficult this is can be observed from the majority of battle scenes, which become thoroughly confusing from the moment that the two sides engage. Thus, even in its original form, the Russian *War and Peace*, which was made with apparently limitless resources, falls down completely at Borodino, where we are shown plenty of spectacular action but given little idea of what is actually happening. This confusion cannot really be justified by the fact that the characters don't know what is happening, for we are anyway shown much more than they can possibly know about.

Vittorio Cottafavi, three years after *Hercules Conquers Atlantis*, went on to make a medieval picture with a Spanish setting, *The Hundred Horsemen* (his last film to date). José Luis Guarner has re-

Vittorio Cottafavi's *100 Horsemen*

The War Lord **(1965) starring Charlton Heston, seen here with Richard Boone.**

marked that in its mixture of comedy and tragedy, the picture is very close to Elizabethan theatre. He has described the background to the action, which takes place in a Spanish village around the year 1000 A.D.: 'The peasants are working the land and trying to trick their overlords who, in their turn, are occupied with exploiting the peasants; each side is trying to gain the maximum profit at the other's expense. One day the Arabs arrive. They are organized, disciplined, logical people, and they oppose the disorganization of the Lords and the peasants with intelligence, order, and hard work. These two completely different conceptions of life cannot help but clash, above all because the intellectual superiority of the Arabs stimulates their desire to dominate their weaker neighbours. Two other human groups observe this duel from a distance: the Bandits, whose sole problem is survival and who steal democratically from Christians and Arabs alike, and the Monks, who are seeking truth by means of sacrifice and prayer. The tension between the two great opposing forces results in a fight to the death into which everyone is dragged. . . .' This grass-roots struggle for survival and power is a long way from the chivalrous conflicts that are the stock-in-trade of most medieval pictures. For once, the Middle Ages are played for real rather than as a jolly charade, and our feeling for the characters is sufficiently strong to make the final battle one in which we are emotionally involved, rather than just so much 'sound and fury'. As the casualties mount, Cottafavi achieves an extraordinary effect of desolation by slowly draining the colour away from the image – this

Medieval forces mass in *El Cid* (1961).

Burt Lancaster with a sullen
Virginia Mayo in
The Flame And The Arrow (1950).

Kay Kendall and Robert Taylor in
The Adventures Of Quentin Durward
(1956).

Burt Lancaster in *The Crimson Pirate*
(1952).

Prince Valiant **(1953) starred Robert Wagner.**

Tony Curtis and Janet Leigh in
The Black Shield Of Falworth **(1954).**

Stephen Boyd in
The Fall Of The Roman Empire **(1964).**

only works because of the power the film has already generated; without that, it would seem very calculated.

In the popular cinema, the only film that I can remember coming near to *The Hundred Horsemen* in the strength of its depiction of medieval life is Franklin Schaffner's *The War Lord*, although it is centrally concerned with only two characters, the Lord and his squire, Charlton Heston and Richard Boone. On a grand scale, of course, a very satisfactory treatment of the struggle against the Moors in Spain is to be found in *El Cid*, although it is sometimes submerged in the pictorial beauty of the images and the conscious grandeur of the effects.

The strong suit of most medieval pictures, though, has not been historical interest but humour. Even Richard Thorpe, who made a number of rather colourless historical movies in the 50s, managed a few jolly moments in his *Quentin Durward*, which has a trapped Kay Kendall frantically feeling around the walls of a castle chamber, saying that 'there has to be a secret passage somewhere'. The Middle Ages have one legend that has always attracted the movies: that of Robin Hood. Its most notable screen appearance was in the Douglas Fairbanks version, directed by Allan Dwan, but a splendid variant appeared in Jacques Tourneur's *The Flame and the Arrow*, one of the two films which really capitalized on the extrovert, acrobatic talents of the young Burt Lancaster (the other was Robert Siodmak's *The Crimson Pirate*). Even the glum presence of Virginia Mayo as the leading lady cannot damp the lively spirits of its band of lovable outlaws; the jollity even survives the obviously studio-shot exteriors which have to do duty as Europe. The acrobatics give the film one of the most beautiful of all closing shots: Lancaster swinging in a series of circular movements on metalwork high above the courtyard of a castle.

The Flame and the Arrow does not even have the very tenuous connections with history that Robin Hood has. The benefits of such freedom from encumbering fact are to be seen in two of the best pre-Renaissance romps, Henry Hathaway's *Prince Valiant* and Rudolph Maté's *The Black Shield of Falworth*. These two films have another point in common: their heroes are two of the most American of film stars, respectively Robert Wagner and Tony Curtis (and for good measure *Prince Valiant*, which is based on a comic strip, has another quintessentially American actor, Sterling Hayden as Sir Galahad). In both films, the heroes start off more-or-less as yokels in the sophisticated world of knighthood, surviving by their native wit against minor heavies like Patrick O'Neal in *The Black Shield of Falworth* until they are able to take on the major league heavies like O'Neal's kinsman, David Farrar. In medieval movies, the British actors tend to play the experienced old hands (here Torin Thatcher and Herbert Marshall) or the sophisticated villains (such as Farrar) while the American accents of heroes like Wagner and Curtis are used to demonstrate lack of courtly polish – Wagner has a tendency early in *Prince Valiant* to fall off his horse. Their gaucheness combined with their youthfully eager personalities makes them a winning pair of heroes, both potential giant-killers.

Genevieve Bujold as Anne Boleyn in
Anne Of The Thousand Days (1970).

Renaissance processions from
The Agony And The Ecstasy (1965)
starring Charlton Heston as
Michaelangelo.

Charlton Heston in
The Agony & the Ecstasy.

TUDOR FACES:
Genevieve Bujold as
Anne Of The Thousand Days **(1970).**

Glenda Jackson as Elizabeth I in
Mary Of Scots.
Florence Eldridge as Elizabeth I in
John Ford's *Mary Of Scotland* **(1936).**

Katherine Hepburn as
Mary Of Scotland.
Vanessa Redgrave as
Mary Queen Of Scots.

Merle Oberon as Anne Boleyn
in Alexander Korda's
The Private Life Of Henry VIII **(1932).**

Charles Laughton as Henry VIII in
The Private Life Of Henry VIII.

Richard Burton as Henry VIII in
Anne Of The Thousand Days.

87

SWASHBUCKLING DAYS:
Douglas Fairbanks in
The Three Musketeers.

Stewart Granger and Mel Ferrer in
Scaramouche.

Jean Peters as *Anne Of The Indies.*

Errol Flynn and Basil Rathbone in
Captain Blood.

The Renaissance has proved very much less of an inspiration than the Middle Ages, lending itself to treatments that are more pretentious than stimulating, more talkative than active. There is *The Agony and the Ecstasy*, from a novel by Irving Stone (who also gave us the Vincent van Gogh story in 'Lust for Life'), with Charlton Heston as Michelangelo and Rex Harrison as Pope Julius II. No more inspiring as a source are the Maxwell Anderson plays, which have had a considerable influence on the screen image of the Tudors from *Mary of Scotland* and *The Private Lives of Elizabeth and Essex* to *Anne of the Thousand Days*. With the possible exception of Alexander Korda's *The Private Life of Henry VIII*, which does offer Charles Laughton doing his spirited impersonation of the Merry Monarch, the Renaissance has on the whole been one of the cinema's dark ages.

In the seventeenth and eighteenth centuries, however, the literary sources become at least livelier, for these two centuries, and particularly the period from Louis XIV to the French Revolution, were much favoured by later popular novelists from Alexandre Dumas *père* onwards. From the appearance of 'The Three Musketeers' in 1844, his simplified but flamboyant vision has shaped popular ideas of French history. The transference of this sort of swashbuckling tale to the cinema produces movies that have much in common with musicals, with action sequences such as swordfights taking the place of dance numbers – the two forms are combined in Vincente Minnelli's swashbuckling musical *The Pirate*. It's not surprising, then, that two of the best swashbuckling pictures were made by a director best known for musicals, George Sidney, with *The Three Musketeers* (which had Gene Kelly as d'Artagnan) and *Scaramouche*, from Rafael Sabatini. Both films have a quick rhythm and a nimble grace that is almost choreographic.

The other characteristic that swashbucklers share with musicals is innocence. They form a genre that is notable for its lack of self-consciousness, which extends to the three main varieties – French and royalist (like *The Three Musketeers*), British and naval (*Captain Horatio Hornblower*) or Caribbean and piratical (of which my favourite is Jacques Tourneur's *Anne of the Indies*). Where the musical has survived at all only by changing, the swashbuckler has simply vanished – we have yet to be treated to the adult swashbuckler.

CHAPTER 7

MANIPULATION AND PROPAGANDA

When *Dr No* was first released, I was rebuked in print by Ian Fleming for using the term 'fascist' in connection with James Bond. Fleming apparently thought of his hero's politics as being, if anything, left of centre. Bond's behaviour, though, is a different matter, particularly when it is magnified on the screen. As their operations are supposedly crucial to the security of the Western Alliance if not to the survival of democracy, Bond and his derivatives enjoy the privileged position of being able to do absolutely anything they like. The trick in Bond was the OO 'licensed to kill' label which gave a veneer of justification to all the screwing (not shown but leeringly suggested) and the mayhem.

As a film hero, Bond is in no way preferable and in essence little different to the aggressive commie bashers like John Wayne in *Big Jim McLain* who were such an affront to liberal spirits of two decades ago. Indeed one might prefer Big Jim and his contemporaries on the grounds that there was at least some degree of sincerity behind their conception, for if there is anything of which one can be sure it is that John Wayne really doesn't like communists. The spy movies, on the other hand, were totally cynical confections, at least until the late and almost uniformly catastrophic attempts to bring integrity and therefore gloom to the genre – most of these were adaptations of the then fashionable novels of John le Carré such as Sidney Lumet's *The Deadly Affair* and Martin Ritt's soporific *The Spy Who Came in from the Cold.*

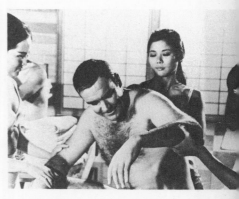

The saving grace of Bond and co. for the film critics of the 60s was the knowing tongue-in-cheek treatment, a spurious consolation as it only showed that those involved did not believe in what they were up to. The appeal of spy movies to the public, though, depends more on the suaveness with which the thug hero carries his invincibility. The early 50s anti-communist movies were mainly modestly budgeted affairs which were not an outstanding success at the box-office. The Bond films took the ostensibly patriotic violence out of the crummy locales of the police movie to place it in all the luxury of a high-budget Universal weepie. The winning combination at the box-office was dream-land luxury plus vicarious sex and violence.

You Only Live Twice **(1967).**
Sean Connery as James Bond.

In many ways, Bond is the gentlemanly British cousin of Mickey Spillane's hero Mike Hammer. However, Hammer is a freelance working in an uneasy relationship with the law which is bureaucratically scrupulous at the expense of dynamism, whereas Bond has joined a big organization, the Establishment, which gives him the license to go through much the same motions in ritzier surroundings and provides him with the weaponry to escalate his firepower. The best film about Hammer, Robert Aldrich's *Kiss Me, Deadly*, was a critique of Spillane, keeping the audience constantly aware that Hammer is SuperHeel; indirectly it was a film against McCarthyism.

Bond movies, on the other hand, present 007 in a totally uncritical light. There is very little to disturb the audience's enjoyment of Bond's prowess in sex and violence; we may be stirred but we are never shaken. As they have no other line, one might expect the Bond pictures to play up their exploitable elements for all they are worth. But even within their chosen limits (those of a British A

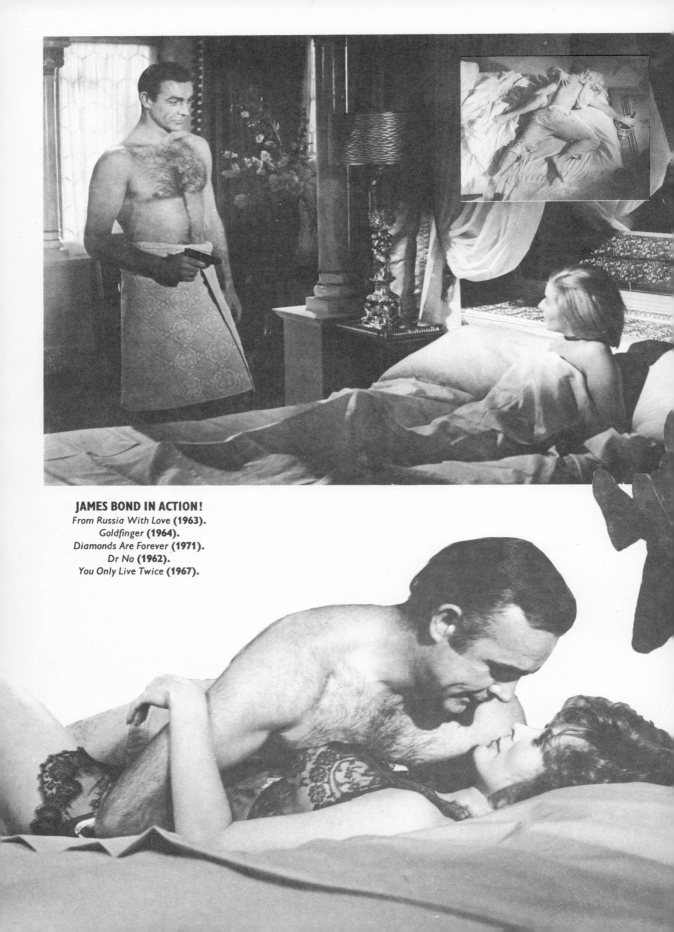

JAMES BOND IN ACTION!
From Russia With Love **(1963).**
Goldfinger **(1964).**
Diamonds Are Forever **(1971).**
Dr No **(1962).**
You Only Live Twice **(1967).**

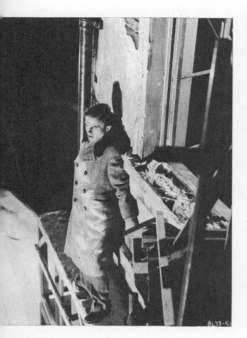

James Mason in *The Man Between* (1953).

The Spy Who Came In From The Cold (1965) with Richard Burton, and *The Deadly Affair* (1967) attempting to show a wetter, harsher reality in the world of espionage than the dream-land luxury of the world of Bond.

Certificate – a more restricted censor rating would start to cut down the potential audience), they are curiously tame. The violence is half-hearted, the sex jaded, and the reliance on gadgetry rather than straightforward action seems symptomatic of middle age and waning virility (making the success of the Bond movies indicative of the decline of the cinema). However, I have heard it argued that some justification for the Bond movies is to be found in their very tepidness, that they function as a form of psychotherapy, a means for the audience to work out violent or anti-social impulses at a very low temperature. Even if it did offer a tiny safety valve for society, the spy cycle was as sterile a development as any that the cinema has produced, and its gadgetry was so elaborately and knowingly contrived that one cannot even see it offering nostalgic inspiration to some future artist, as the 40s space serials did to, say, Eduardo Paolozzi.

The war movie is also something of a problem on the level of content. In the days of 'committed' film criticism, which meant heart-on-sleeve socio-political attitudes ranging from the 50s New Left to weedier brands of liberalism, much airing was given to the idea of the 'anti-war' film. The concept was not particularly valuable, as a movie which devotes its energies to demonstrating what a perfectly rotten show war is for all concerned is not likely to reward the viewer by the richness of its expression. In any case, there is a great danger that the adventure element that is almost inseparable from the scenes of action will zap the pacifism, giving the proceedings, which are supposed to be turning us off war, a distinctly positive quality of excitement. There are very few films which manage to avoid attributing any value at all to war. One is Jean-Luc Godard's *Les Carabiniers* which uses all the aids to detachment that the director can muster in order to destroy the coherence of the action and to remove from war even the value of an emotional experience.

The excitement of action can be found even in the most prestigious of 'anti-war' movies from *All Quiet on the Western Front* to *Paths of Glory*. In inferior examples, the sentiments which the audience is supposed to be buying appear only in the dialogue. J. Lee Thompson's *The Guns of Navarone*, David Lean's *Bridge on the River Kwai* and Donald Siegel's *Hell is for Heroes* all contain the simple moral that war is futile and degrading. All three use one of the basic war film gambits: the strategic action of great importance which devolves on a very few men. Of the three, only *Hell is for Heroes* manages to be consistent.

The Guns of Navarone sets out with the obvious intention of telling a rattling good yarn about the way our chaps battled heroically against overwhelming odds to knock out the Jerry guns. Even this it almost fails to do by disastrously overplaying its suspense potential in a lengthy sequence of dud thrills as the team crawl up a crumbling cardboard cliff so early in the movie that all present will obviously have to survive in order to justify their billing on the credits. However, its worst sin is stopping off at least twice in the course of the narrative for dialogue meditations on the nastiness of war, which

94

YOU ARE LEAVING
THE AMERICAN SECTOR
ВЫ ВЫЕЗЖАЕТЕ ИЗ
АМЕРИКАНСКОГО СЕКТОРА
VOUS SORTEZ
DU SECTEUR AMERICAIN
SIE VERLASSEN DEN AMERIKANISCHEN SEKTOR

Soldat-
auch Du bist eingesperrt!

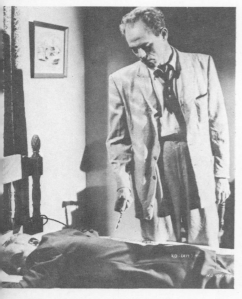

Superheel – Mickey Spillane's
Mike Hammer in *Kiss Me Deadly*
(1955).

the audience is meant to accept and which would in themselves be perfectly sympathetic, if slightly superfluous, in a film that refused to present war as enjoyable. But here their effect is completely vitiated by the rest of the action, and in context they seem almost hypocritical. The friendliest explanation one can offer of this is a lack of firm control in the overall conception by Lee Thompson and, crucially, by the writer-producer Carl Foreman. Even the one moment which could hardly help having some force, the shooting of Gia Scala as a collaborator, manages not to have any in the film. The script sidesteps here by letting Irene Papas, who is only a secondary character and a Greek anyway, do the shooting, forestalling Gregory Peck and David Niven who would both be more directly affected by the responsibility for Gia Scala's death. The lack of conviction is almost total.

Hell is for Heroes is based on a story by Robert Pirosh which could easily have turned into a plug for the gallantry of the American fighting man, like that William Wellman made more than a decade earlier from a Pirosh story in *Battleground*. I am not concerned here with the central theme in the film which is embodied in the Steve McQueen character, the psychopath who makes an ideal soldier but goes to pieces outside the field of combat (although this theme is entirely consistent with the rest of the film).

A couple of sequences in the film show how the staging of the action is handled without producing the aching inconsistency of *The Guns of Navarone*. In one sequence, three soldiers set out at night on a manoeuvre to trick the enemy into thinking that large patrols are being sent out and that therefore the front is well manned. The idea is to take empty ammunition tins out into no-man's land, fill them with stones and rattle them by remote control using lengths of telephone wire, when they are back at their position. The noise of the cans would be picked up by the enemy's ground microphones and all hell would be let loose to greet the ghost patrol. Siegel does not tell us what the three soldiers are doing until their mission is almost completed. We take the episode seriously, which is right because it is serious, and no less dangerous than a real patrol. If we had been shown beforehand exactly what the three men were up to, the sequence would have been invested with a feeling, as we sit safely in our cinema seats, that here is a piece of fun, fooling the enemy.

The final sequence of the film sums up the whole action, in its picture of the smallness of the contribution an individual can make in an infantry battle. Steve McQueen, in serious trouble after leading an abortive attack on a crucial pillbox which has resulted in the death of two of his men, takes it upon himself to put the pillbox out of action. By a suicidal run, he manages to get close enough to lob a satchel charge into the mouth of the box. Inevitably, he is shot. Seeing the charge thrown out of the pillbox, he staggers forward, grabs it and rolls into the mouth of the box with it as it explodes. A flame-thrower is played on the opening to make sure that nobody will survive in it. The last shot of the film starts as a longshot of a general advance beginning along the section of the

Les *Carabiniers* **(1963),
Jean-Luc Godard's anti-war film.**

**The excitement of action is still in
evidence in such famous anti-war
films as** *All Quiet On The Western Front*
and *Paths Of Glory* **(1958).**

The Guns Of Navarone **(1961). The interrogation of Gia Scala with Anthony Quinn, Gregory Peck, David Niven and Stanley Baker.**

Hell Is For Heroes **(1962) with Steve McQueen.**

Bridge On The River Kwai **(1957).**

front around the pillbox. The advance is obviously going to be very costly. The camera zooms in to the mouth of the pillbox and the end title is superimposed. The zoom in from the general view to the detail emphasized the smallness of the gain from McQueen's death. One pillbox has been silenced, and as the advance continues, that pillbox ceases to have any significance. It is left behind, a dead, almost abstract object. Here there is no conflict between the intended content of the film and the form which expresses it.

Contrast the last shot of *Hell is for Heroes* with the end of *Bridge on the River Kwai*. James Donald stands surveying the wreckage of the bridge which was successfully built and has now been successfully blown up. 'Madness, madness,' he says, and the camera soars back away from him in a mood of triumph which is taken up by the martial music on the soundtrack. The sentiments expressed by the dialogue and the meaning contained in the treatment cancel each other out.

The problem of content crops up in a different way in films made for propaganda reasons. Particularly in times of war, the entertainment film can become an important vehicle for propaganda. Documentary demonstrations of the military strength of the home side or of the enemy's beastliness are not going to attract audiences for long – it is notable that in both world wars only the Germans made any number of documentaries celebrating the might of their forces, and they were never the most subtle propagandists. Lack of concern for audience response is entirely consistent with the political stance

British World War II movies created a great feeling of group spirit as exemplified in films like *In Which We Serve*, written, produced by and starring Noel Coward (1942). The most potent of group spirit images, the lifeboat, links films such as *Western Approaches* (1944) and *Lifeboat* (1943).

Harry Watt's *Target For Tonight* (1941).

One Of Our Aircraft Is Missing (1942) and *Five Graves To Cairo* (1943) were made at periods during World War II when all was not going well for the Allies.

Erich Von Stroheim, the director, appearing in *Five Graves To Cairo* as Rommel.

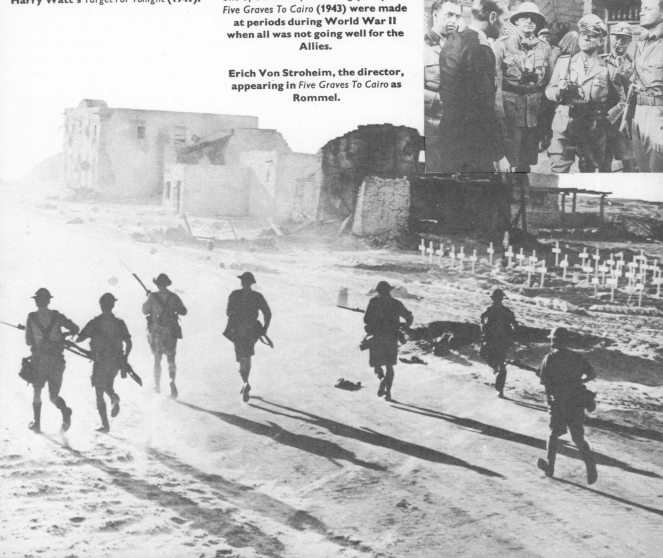

of Nazism. Propaganda becomes more effective if the audiences actually want to see it, and during World War II in Britain and America there was an insatiable appetite for the movies, which offered an available and engulfing form of escape at a time when most other forms were off the menu.

Naturally enough, the opportunity for presenting propaganda in an attractive guise was seized upon with some gusto by both sides. Even outside periods of total war, the thread of propaganda has run through the history of the cinema. The Nazi party in Germany was quick to use the cinema – 1933 saw the release of three Nazi feature films. This interest was not surprising, as Joseph Goebbels, the Minister of Propaganda, according to Leif Furhammar and Folke Isaksson in their book *Politics and Film*, was a man with a dream: 'When the war had been safely won, he planned to devote himself to a theoretical work on film that was to be as crucial to the development of the cinema as Lessing's *Die Hamburgische Dramaturgie* had been to Romantic drama.'

The relationship between propaganda and the entertainment film has been explored in admirable detail by Furhammar and Isaksson, who have uncovered various general principles. They note, for example, that film propaganda is most effective when it reinforces or moulds existing attitudes (just as wish-fulfilment movies draw their strength from dreams that already exist among the audiences). As a means of conversion, the cinema's power is strictly limited.

In the setting of, say, an adventure story, all sorts of attitudes can be strengthened in the minds of the spectators. All the weapons of desire and satisfaction, identification and suspense can be turned to this purpose. British movies were notably successful in fostering a feeling of togetherness against the common foe, a national team spirit. The British cinema was filled with images representing the great spirit of the group (us) which allows it to survive through hardships and struggles, like the destroyer crew of *In Which We Serve*. The most potent of the group spirit images was that of the lifeboat, which links this film with Pat Jackson's *Western Approaches* and Alfred Hitchcock's *Lifeboat*. There are also films like Harry Watt's *Target for Tonight*, which present group action in which individual identities are completely submerged – people are identified by the tasks they perform (the film is documentary fiction using real airmen rather than actors).

The German cinema offered more extrovert images of comradeship among the troops united in the communal joy of serving their Führer and building the Greater Reich. Where British films were showing a spirit of survival and resistance, the Germans went for heroism and sacrifice. Here Leif Furhammar notes: 'Love was conceded as a positive factor and propaganda stories were structured to subordinate it to something even more elevated – loyalty to Hitler and death for the fatherland. If two sympathetic young men compete for the affections of the same blonde girl in a Nazi movie, it may well be fascinating to discover who gets her, but for example in Gustav Ucicky's *Morgenrot* (*Dawn*, 1933) . . . it is the rejected suitor who becomes the undisputed hero by winning a prize greater

than a woman's love: heroic martyrdom, the intrinsic emotional value of which is here heightened by the love interest.'

The propaganda movie in World War II had to adjust itself to the fluctuating fortunes of the combatants. Early in a war, it is possible, though somewhat hazardous, to encourage optimism by playing down the strength of the enemy – one or two Russian movies made before the outbreak of hostilities show the border defences having little difficulty in repelling the invaders. At points when the war was clearly not going well, various British and American movies including Michael Powell's *One of our Aircraft is Missing* and Billy Wilder's *Five Graves to Cairo* end on the note of forthcoming return to territories which have fallen into the hands of the Germans.

On the whole, it is a good idea for the propagandist to show the other side as the one which does all the killing. But sooner or later, our side has to hit back, which presents the problem of how to retain sympathy for our lads now that they are doing the killing. This is particularly important when you are involved in some operation like crushing Poland. Gustav Ucicky's *Heimkehr* (*Homecoming*, 1941) got round this problem by first painting a savage picture of the Polish terror directed against German minorities, in order to provide a retrospective justification for the German invasion in 1939 – in the film this arrives in the nick of time as a group of the embattled minority are to be drowned by the Polish heavies for listening to a broadcast of a speech by Hitler.

When the killing and torture come down to an individual level, even more nimble footwork is required. Leif Furhammar found a couple of instances in Zoltan Korda's *Sahara* (1943): when 'our boys are about to use force on their prisoners, the cowardly fellows spill everything straight away. There is then no need for further brutality, and no slur on our heroes' morality. . . . There is, in the same film, another elaborate variation on the rationalization of violence, perhaps the most common. When the enemy leader quite simply has to be killed, for plot and audience-manipulation reasons, by someone on our side, the murder is committed by a Sudanese in a fit of blind rage: violence on the good side is almost exclusively perpetrated by individuals who are definitely allies but somehow not the same as us. We do not have to regard them as our representatives.' (An identical gambit is the killing of Gia Scala by Irene Papas in *The Guns of Navarone*.)

The great ally of the propagandist is history, for with a little bit of doctoring if necessary it will furnish precedents for almost anything. Current leaders may acquire glory from it – John F. Kennedy's war record was celebrated in a feeble picture called *PT 109* – but more usually they are built up through carefully drawn parallels with their greatest antecedents. There are some pretty discreet efforts in this line from the Allies – parallels can be found to Roosevelt in Henry King's *Wilson* (1944) and to Churchill in Carol Reed's *The Young Mr Pitt* (1942). The spectacular example here is Hitler, who may be seen by implication in a couple of films about Bismarck and quite a number on Frederick the Great.

Historical parallels may be used to call up omens of success for

German propaganda films showed troops united in the common joy of serving their Fuhrer and the Reich . . . Gustav Ucicky's *Morgenrot* (1933) and *Heimkehr* (1941).

In World War II historic parallels
were used by most countries to
conjure up omens of success, as in
Wilson (1944) in the USA,
The Young Mr Pitt (1942) in Britain, and
Scipio Africanus in Italy.

**Success against
Napoleon in the past was a constant
source of encouragement for
practically everyone.**

**Nelson in *Lady Hamilton* (1941)
– Britain.**

General Suvorov **(1941) and** Kutuzov
– Russia.

**E. Jannings in the German film about
Frederick The Great,**
Der Alte Und Der Junge Koenig.

Kolberg **(1945) – Germany.**

current actions. Thus Carmine Gallone's Roman epic *Scipio Africanus* (1937) was clearly referring to Mussolini's attempts at colonizing Africa. When Hitler was on the attack, the Russians produced a number of comforting reminders of their defeat of Napoleon such as Pudovkin's *Suvorov* (1940). Success against Napoleon was a recurrent source of encouragement – *Suvorov* and Vladimir Petrov's *Kutuzov* for the Russians, *The Young Mr Pitt* and Nelson (for example in Alexander Korda's *Lady Hamilton* (1941)) for the British, and Veit Harlan's *Kolberg* (1945) for the Germans. This was the last film to be produced at the bidding of Dr Goebbels. In the days when Germany was moving towards defeat, this colour film about a garrison town holding out to the last against Napoleon and being miraculously saved was calculated to inspire new fortitude in the Germans.

The principle of using history or historical legend for political ends did not start with World War II. Even D. W. Griffith back in 1922 was using the French Revolution as a ghastly warning against the danger of the Russian Revolution in *Orphans of the Storm*. Decidedly, history has taken a battering at the hands of the cinema: when it is not being distorted for political ends, it is likely to be reduced to the level of simple fun.

Dorothy and Lillian Gish in D. W. Griffith's *Orphans Of The Storm* (1922).

CHAPTER 8

THE ADVENTURERS

Outside the humble confines of the serial and the B-western the cinema has produced very few long-running characters whose fortunes are followed eagerly from one picture to the next. In adventure movies, none of James Bond's descendants managed to survive for more than two or three appearances (except, of course, the Men from UNCLE who had the support of a successful television series). The sword and bosom department has had one relatively long-running bosom in Angélique, who was played by Michèle Mercier in at least four undistinguished romps through Revolutionary and Napoleonic France. But far outlasting all other characters in the cinema is Tarzan, whose appearances have run all the way from silent serials to a television series which had Ron Ely, one of the most satisfactory performers, in the title part.

It is difficult to see why Tarzan has proved such a durable film hero. Even without his entourage of Jane, the chimpanzee Cheetah and an optional small boy, Tarzan is an amazingly improbable figure, a one-man vigilante squad of the jungle, combining the carefully nourished physique of an athletic champion with an unequalled talent for tuning in to nature: the animals (at least the nice ones) are his friends and the creepers which he uses for swinging from tree to tree never break under his weight. In the simplified ecosystem of the studio forest, Tarzan occupies a special niche of non-predatory dominance.

One might suggest a number of reasons for his appeal to audiences. Most obviously, he is a symbol of freedom: swinging along unencumbered by western clothing, he appears to lead a life of natural contentment, as well he might in an environment of tropical warmth without the usually attendant ministrations of the mosquito and tsetse fly – it seems either health hazards are absent from Tarzan's particular jungle or else he has a blanket immunity to everything from malaria to bilharziasis. Indeed, one might view Tarzan's kingdom as a secular version of the Garden of Eden without the Almighty to screw things up, a garden in which none of the fruit is forbidden.

A second possible strand of appeal, though one that is largely negated by the aseptic personas of the two main sound-era Tarzans, Johnny Weissmuller and Lex Barker, is sex – one might expect some of Tarzan's physical vigour to show up in this department. Usually, however, he shows himself to be one of nature's gentlemen.

Tarzan also has a more dubious area of appeal: he is the ultimate symbol of white supremacy. He is a white man who can beat the natives at their own game: living in the jungle without any recourse to the technology of civilization he can be relied upon to get any dissident fuzzies back into line as well as meting out justice to any scoundrelly whites. He is a figure from the days when the white imperialist was still an ideal – it was 1914 when Edgar Rice Burroughs introduced him with *Tarzan Of The Apes*.

Whatever his appeal, Tarzan has lasted best on the screen. In the 60s, when the novels were largely forgotten, the films were still going strong. The series has been through a succession of Tarzans: in the sound era, Johnny Weissmuller made twelve Tarzan movies

Michele Mercier as
Angelique, Marquise des Anges.

THE FIRST FOUR TARZANS:
Former fireman Gene Pollar in
Return Of Tarzan **(1920).**
Kamuela C. Searle as *Son Of Tarzan*
(1920).
James Pierce in
Tarzan And The Golden Lion **(1927).**
Elmo Lincoln, the first
Tarzan Of The Apes **(1918).**

Gordon Scott as *Tarzan The Magnificent* (1960).

Johnny Weissmuller in *Tarzan And His Mate* **(1934)**.

Tarzan The Ape Man –
Johnny Weissmuller (1932).

Tarzan And The She-Devil **(1952) with
Lex Barker as Tarzan, and
Monique Van Vooren and
Raymond Burr.**

Tarzan And The Amazons **(1945).**

**Ron Ely, TV's Tarzan, with
Jill Donahue.**

Football star Mike Henry as Tarzan in the 60s.

Tarzan And The Lost Safari **(1957) with Gordon Scott as Tarzan.**

from 1932 to 1948, and Lex Barker made five (1949–1953); later Tarzans have showed less staying power.

The conception, too, has varied widely from the original *Tarzan, The Ape Man*, in which Weissmuller is discovered in an area of jungle that is taboo to the natives (who have to be soundly whipped by the chief porter before they will enter it). He has apparently not seen a woman before, and knows only the words he picks up in the course of the movie. This is a stroke of luck for Weissmuller who therefore gets through more or less unscathed by Ivor Novello's appalling dialogue. C. Aubrey Smith tells his daughter Jane (Maureen O'Sullivan): 'My dear, he's not like us.' 'He's white.' 'But people like that . . . it doesn't matter that he's white.' But the Tarzan/Jane relationship progresses to the point where she can say to the uncomprehending Ape Man, 'Darling, what are we going to do about us?'

For most of his sound film career, though, Tarzan has been able to talk, and the most recent Tarzan movies, dating from the late 60s, present a very different hero. In *Tarzan And The Great River* he is first seen wearing a lounge suit as he arrives by 'plane to visit his friends at a South American zoo. But the death of the zoo's curator soon has him getting into his loin cloth and setting out after the heavies. In the later Tarzans, it took great ingenuity on the part of the writers to keep the series afloat. The standard of direction had also risen, along with the amount of location shooting, and some of the films were quite efficiently put together by two British directors, John Guillermin and Robert Day.

By far the most spirited of the Tarzan movies, though, was Joseph M. Newman's 1959 remake of *Tarzan, The Ape Man*. This was really a shoestring affair, lapsing into black and white (or rather olive and white) for the longshots of swinging through the jungle, purloined from the Weissmuller version. It also combines an apparently Edwardian setting with a driving jazz score by Shorty Rogers and has a narrator who perishes half way through. It is the only Tarzan movie to make anything of the sexual possibilities of the character (here played by Denny Miller). When Jane (Joanna Barnes), this time a starchy lady missionary, finds herself confronted by his half-naked figure advancing towards her emitting friendly grunts, she gets the idea that his intentions are not entirely honourable. Backing away until there is no escape, she finds comfort in reciting the 23rd Psalm, which acquires some new connotations – 'I shall not want. He maketh me to lie down in green pastures.' Then she passes out.

A curious footnote to the film career of Tarzan comes from Germany. At least since the end of World War II, the German cinema has been among the world's most uninspired. No directors of any real talent emerged in West Germany until the end of the 60s (and even then, they worked outside the normal commercial channels). The German cinema gave every appearance of being totally controlled by the most stolid of businessmen. It was chronically short of ideas, and having no native genres to fall back on, copied whichever imported forms seemed most likely to yield the

Jean-Paul Belmondo –
That Man From Rio **(1963).**

KIRK DOUGLAS
in *Ace In The Hole* **(1950).**
The Heroes Of Telemark **(1965).**
Along The Great Divide **(1951).**

ANTHONY QUINN
in *The Last Train From Gun Hill* **(1958)**.
Warlock **(1959)**.

TYRONE POWER
with Annabella in *Suez* (1938).

Captain From Castile (1947).

with Basil Rathbone in
The Mark Of Zorro (1940).

Mississippi Gambler (1953).

Robert Taylor as *Ivanhoe* **(1952).**

quick Deutschmark. Thus, there were sagas of prostitution in the French manner, though more turgidly moralizing and more recently, Edgar Wallace thrillers and westerns from the pen of the German writer Karl May, whose main two characters were called Winnetou, the Warrior and Old Shatterhand. (The latter is an archetypal western bringer of justice: he makes his first appearance in *Old Shatterhand* (1964) when a band of heavies are conducting an alfresco lynching – he blasts everyone in sight, apart from the victim, and they all rush off into the undergrowth clutching their damaged hands and yelling 'It's Old Shatterhand!')

In casting around for subjects, the Germans seized on Tarzan, who had the defect of being still in copyright, with his film rights sold to Hollywood. Therefore Tarzan was revamped with characteristic thoroughness, and always with an eye for commercial improvements. Thus we get Germany's answer to Tarzan, Liane, who is clearly the result of the thought that such a sparing quantity of clothing could be seen to better advantage on a girl. To please local tastes, she is also very young and very blonde. Of course, she could not manage the wrestling matches with lions, but the spectacle of a near-naked girl swinging through the jungle was sufficiently diverting to sustain her through two or three movies.

In looking at the cinema as a medium for presenting adventure, we have so far largely ignored one aspect which is clearly crucial, the whole business of star personality. Here we are on very treacherous ground, as the personality that emerges from any movie is a combination of the screen image the star has developed during the whole of his career and the approach adopted by the director; the director's approach in turn will be a combination of overt attitudes and the more-or-less subconscious values that shape his vision. Both star and director operate within the limits of the current convention and the demands of the script (and, for that matter, the varying degrees of indifference from the producer or studio), although the personality of one director or the other may well be strong enough to break through the constraints to impose itself as the dominant characteristic of the picture.

Particularly in dealing with adventure movie stars, we are faced with the problem of where to stop: most stars have at one time or another done adventure movies. Even an actor like Jean-Paul Belmondo who seems to belong in or around the seedy milieu of the French crime picture has done adventure movies, usually with a large helping of comedy, like Philippe de Broca's *Cartouche* and Jean-Paul Rappeneau's *Les Maries de l'An II*, both period pictures, and de Broca's *That Man From Rio*, a chase movie that has him executing feats of athletic daring in the skyscraper modernity of Rio de Janeiro and Brasilia. Many of the big American stars spread their activities over a wide range of pictures – a Kirk Douglas or an Anthony Quinn will have made a number of adventure movies, but his screen image will draw on his appearances in many other contexts. Our main concern here will be to look at a few of the stars who have spent much of their careers in the realms of adventure or have become identified with some part of its mythology.

120

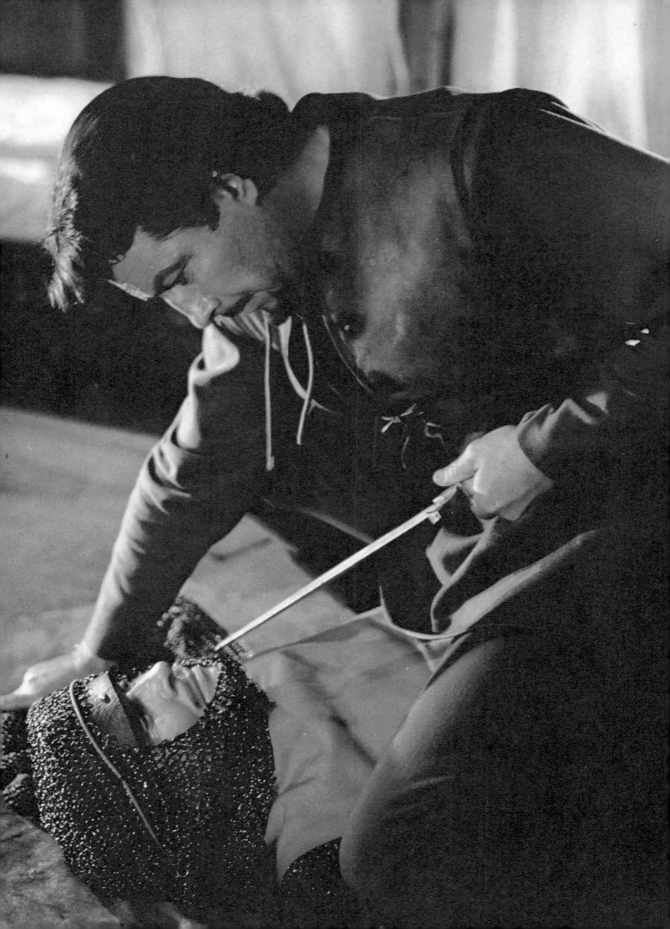

Although the idea of the adventure movie does not lend itself to accurate definition, one can identify a group of particularly characteristic heroes who are variations on the theme of the Adventurer. V. F. Perkins has noted that there are a couple of basic Adventurer stories much used in the cinema and lending themselves to any number of personal approaches. There is the story of the soldier-of-fortune type brought to realization of other values, and a related plot-line which has a hero whose values remain constant through a long series of trials which test their firmness and validity. 'In either case,' Perkins observes, 'the point of the film is not reached at a climax where the hero either affirms or rejects the values he has lived by: the point lies in the testing of his beliefs right through the movie.' In this context, the personality projected by the hero will give weight to his values – it is through his behaviour rather than through direct statements that these will come across most effectively to the audience.

ALAN LADD
being whipped by Brian Donlevy in
Two Years Before The Mast **(1945):**

Even in the upper reaches of stardom, though, there are actors who are very competent professional performers but add nothing to their roles as they appear in the scripts – possibly the most notable of them were Tyrone Power and Alan Ladd. A film like Henry King's *Captain From Castile* is not undermined by the presence of Power in the star part (though it is by a lack of moral fibre *vis-à-vis* the operations of Cortez and his men) – there is nothing much to fault his performance. Yet with a star who could bring some power of his own to the part, the film would have been much stronger. It would also have been different – it would have reflected the personality of its star, and probably would have required modifications in the script to accommodate him.

in the title role of *The Black Knight*
(1954).

with Van Heflin in *The Badlanders*
(1958).

Some stars who customarily play heroes are at their best when they are not entirely good guys. Gregory Peck, for example is at his least interesting when he is displaying uncomplicated integrity. His considerable charm can be put to better use in comedies, like Vincente Minelli's *Designing Woman* or Stanley Donen's *Arabesque*, or by combining it with a total lack of principle as in King Vidor's *Duel In The Sun*, or at least with a degree of roguery as in *How The West Was Won*. Robert Taylor, whose charm was distinctly sleazier than Peck's, could be very colourless when he had to play the heroes of MGM spectaculars; in the rougher settings, as in *Westward The Women* in which he leads a wagon train of husband-hungry women to California, he could offer a suitably hard-bitten performance. Again, he was at his best as a heavy as the cheerful villain of Richard Brooke's *The Last Hunt*.

The style of acting that goes with the Adventurer has been characterized by Perkins with great accuracy as being massive and representational but not detailed and realistic. At the simplest and least interesting level, the Adventurer is represented by the athletic extroversion of Douglas Fairbanks whose appeal lay in his lighter-than-air agility which he presented with a degree of flamboyant display and great good humour. The most splendid performer in this vein, though, was Burt Lancaster, particularly in Jacques Tourneur's *The Flame And The Arrow* and its more lavish successor, Robert

Gregory Peck as
Captain Horatio Hornblower **(1951).**

123

GREGORY PECK
with Sophia Loren in *Arabesque* **(1966).**
Duel In The Sun **(1946) with**
Jennifer Jones.

Siodmak's *The Crimson Pirate*. In these films, possibly thanks in part to having sound to help him, but largely because he is physically a lot more impressive than Fairbanks, Lancaster has a far more powerful screen presence. All those teeth in his flashing shark-like smile radiate complete confidence in his physical prowess and Machiavellian cunning. Between Fairbanks and Lancaster, the main exponent of athletic adventure was, regrettably, Errol Flynn. He was never a particularly talented actor – his efforts at coping with Maxwell Anderson's carefully written lines in *The Private Lives of Elizabeth And Essex* are frequently embarrassing, although he did improve and by *Objective Burma* was at least adequate. Although he was physically right for the swashbuckling parts, he seemed able to do little more than go through the motions of flamboyance – what he fatally lacked was warmth. His narrow-eyed, thin-lipped look could never communicate the exuberance of Fairbanks or Lancaster.

Robert Taylor in *Quo Vadis* (1951).

with John McIntire in *Ambush* (1950).

The 50s, which were more-or-less the end of the road for the simple period adventure movies, offered several variants on the Adventurer hero. For plain integrity, there was Rock Hudson in his more rudimentary pictures for Universal such as *The Desert Hawk* and *The Golden Blade*. Hudson's screen personality, though, also contains a certain softness which fitted him to play the young gambler in Anthony Mann's *Bend Of The River*, a flashy dresser who is quick with a gun but is warned by Arthur Kennedy that his habit of not shooting to kill will get him into trouble one day. This softness was later brilliantly exploited by Douglas Sirck in *The Tarnished Angels,* in which Hudson was a local newspaper reporter obsessed by the apparently glamorous lives of racing pilots and parachutists. Many of his parts in the 50s could well have been written with Gregory Peck in mind. Thus Raoul Walsh's *The Lawless Breed* with Hudson is clearly indebted to Henry King's *The Gunfighter* with Peck. Both have heroes who are redeemed gunfighters willing to sacrifice themselves to prevent their sons from following in their footsteps. One could equally see Peck instead of Hudson in the leading parts of, say, *Battle Hymn, Giant* and *A Farewell To Arms.*

Douglas Fairbanks in *The Three Musketeers.*

An adventure film which allowed him to display an honest impudence of his own was Douglas Sirck's delightful Irish picture *Captain Lightfoot*, in which he is a rebel lad whose activities against the English take him into their smart gaming-rooms patronized by the military and their aristocratic allies. The boyish mischief of Hudson here and its slightly harder equivalent in Burt Lancaster are paralleled by a sort of gutter-snipe impudence from Robert Wagner in *Prince Valiant* and Tony Curtis in *The Prince Who Was A Thief* and *The Black Shield Of Falworth*. (More recently, boyish charm has been one of the main resources of Steve McQueen, who uses his cute smile with such frequency and calculation in films where he is meant to be likeable that it becomes quite irksome.)

A much more resilient – and in the long run more popular – quality in Adventurer heroes is rugged experience. This may show itself in flinty determination bordering on disillusionment, the mood of Richard Boone in Joseph M. Newman's *A Thunder Of Drums*. An ageing cavalry officer, widowed and passed over for

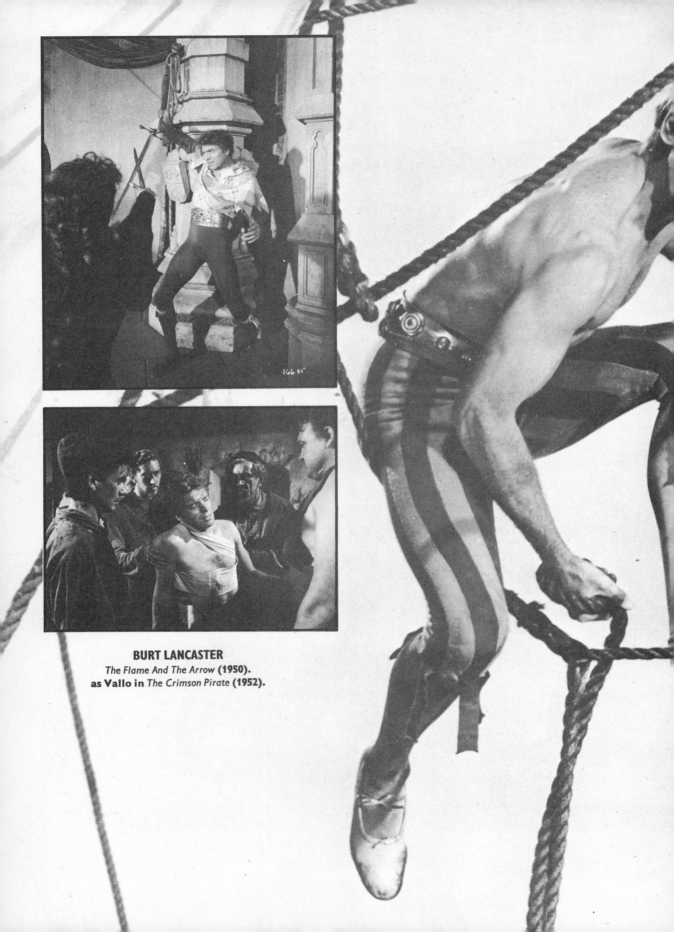

BURT LANCASTER
The Flame And The Arrow **(1950).**
as Vallo in *The Crimson Pirate* **(1952).**

promotion in an army that is his entire life, he goes on inexorably working to raise his whole garrison to his own unbending level of devotion to duty. Bachelors, he believes, make the best officers: they have nothing to lose but their loneliness. But where despair has not set in, the veteran Adventurers have an essentially conservative but still sympathetic sense of what is fitting, as well as a complementary awareness of their own resources, both internal and external, and of just how far they will stretch. In the 50s, Joel McCrea and Randolph Scott belonged to this category, as did the much more gaunt figure of Gary Cooper in *Man Of The West*.

But the actor who has most successfully exploited an image of experience and reliability is John Wayne, whose current screen persona seems to date from 1959 or 1960, respectively the years of *Rio Bravo* and *North To Alaska*. In *Rio Bravo*, he perfected the gruff self-reliance that was already identifiable in, say, *The Searchers* (1956), but was to be the keynote of his later movies; here, too, is an early instance of the skill at deploying resources which turns up again in, for example, *The War Wagon* and *Rio Lobo*. *North To Alaska*, an action comedy directed by Henry Hathaway, opened up another side of the latter-day Wayne image, the petty irritability that leads up to the comic fisticuffs in John Ford's *Donovan's Reef* and in Andrew McLaglen's *McLintock!*; both of these pictures culminate with Wayne soundly spanking the heroines, an action which we are supposed to believe will bring the errant female to her senses, which means, improbably, into renewed devotion to her chastizer. In many ways, *McLintock!* is the definitive portrait of Wayne in the 60s, a film made entirely under his control and without the complications of an important director or male co-stars to steal the limelight. Here, as in the later *Chisum*, we get a glimpse of Wayne's political side – in both films he is a cattle baron and represents the pleasures of success in the bracing atmosphere of *laissez-faire* capitalism. In *McLintock!* someone is asked why he addresses Wayne as 'Sir' and is informed that it's because he has deserved it. *Chisum* is, if anything, even more smug about success, and it starts with Wayne riding up his hill to survey his acres of cattle-filled range. Wayne is one of the very few stars whose screen image seems to be the embodiment of his beliefs.

For Adventurer heroes, youthful vigour is not at a premium, as one might expect. The most characteristic of all variants on the Adventurer hero is even further away than Wayne from such an ideal. He has probably weathered life in surroundings that are more dubious than rugged; he is world-worn, possibly almost cynical, and verging on seediness. But he has been through the mill and survived (though often very much less than triumphantly). Quite often not endowed with much in the way of physical glamour, he is nevertheless one of the central Adventurer figures, perhaps the most important of all, with Clark Gable as his leading exponent.

Some of his appeal may lie in the fact that his actions are not limited by a monumental integrity like that usually displayed by Joel McCrae or Randolph Scott. Unlike these comparatively idealistic figures, he is guided less by duty than by pragmatism and

ROCK HUDSON
Captain Lightfoot **(1954).**
with Jay C. Flippen and Julia Adams
in *Bend Of The River* **(1952).**
Tarnished Angels **(1958).**
Dorothy Maguire and Rock Hudson.
Battle Hymn **(1957).**

Gary Cooper in *Man Of The West*.
Randolph Scott and William Bishop
in *Decision At Sundown*.
Joel McCrea in *Foreign Correspondent*.
Joel McCrea and Dean Stock in
Cattle Drive.

self-interest, which may on occasion turn to clear greed, as in Raoul Walsh's *A King And Four Queens,* in which Gable sets about screwing out of Jo van Fleet's four daughters-in-law the whereabouts of the treasure which she has buried for whichever of her bank-robber sons has survived. Here Gable's likeable but unprincipled rogue meets his match in the cleverest of the daughters-in-law, Eleanor Parker, an actress who may be terrible when she's doing her overwrought emotional number (notably the phoney cripple married to Frank Sinatra in *The Man With The Golden Arm*) but is very good at the same sort of relaxed pragmatism as Gable. Here she outwits everyone to end up with him and the gold. The difference between Scott or McCrea and Gable might be traced back to the contexts of survival that they represent: the pioneering existence of survival against the elements and mainly native adversaries compared to the soldier-of-fortune existence of survival in competitive and often unsavoury societies. The distinction may be to some extent artificial but it emphasizes the central feature of the Gable figure: he has been around. He demands a different sort of respect from that due to the pillars of society represented by the mature John Wayne, a less conformist respect than calling him 'Sir' because he's earned it. The Gable hero is much too independent to settle into a Wayne patriarchal role – where his material wealth seems to give him the visible trappings of a respected citizen, as in *Band Of Angels,* his standards and beliefs still remain his own – and likely to bring him into conflict with society. More often, he is an outsider, a soldier of fortune, who has accumulated little material wealth – quite possibly, he won't know at the start of the movie where his next meal is coming from. But even down on his luck, Gable presented an image of assurance that fitted Robert Ryan's description of his character in *The Tall Men* as being what every boy wants to be and what every man regrets not having been.

Early John Wayne in
The Telegraph Trail **(1933) and with**
Mae Madison, *The Big Stampede* **(1932).**

The values represented by Gable, and by Humphrey Bogart in his adventure parts, are very different, then, from those of Scott or McCrea. They are built up from empirical responses to the situations that confront them and may contain elements of compromise that are likely to be straightened out in the course of the film. In both *Casablanca* and *To Have And Have Not,* Bogart clearly despises the Vichy French, but has chosen to remain in their territory as he has found a liveable existence there. The Bogart Adventurer is very different to the Gable version. Where Gable exudes relaxed self-assurance, Bogart's characters always contain an edgy residue from his days of playing psychopaths – this may be well buried in, say, *The Big Sleep,* but no matter how cool the dialogue, it threatens to break through in moments of anger or desperation. In John Huston's laborious adaptation of *The Treasure Of The Sierra Madre,* it takes over completely, fuelled by the lust for gold.

Pragmatic characters like Bogart and Gable can be shown as having one quality which is heavily curbed in the representatives of straight integrity: sex appeal, albeit of the older-man variety. In fact, both of them became more interesting as actors and as screen personalities in the last fifteen years of their lives (both died before

JOHN WAYNE
McLintock! **(1963) with**
Maureen O'Hara.
Rio Lobo **(1970).**
with Lee Marvin in *The Comancheros*
(1961).
Sands Of Iwo Jima **(1950).**
The Undefeated **(1969).**

CLARK GABLE
Red Dust **(1932) with Jean Harlow.**
Twenty years later with
Ava Gardner in *Mogambo* **(1953).**

The King And Four Queens **(1956).**
Band Of Angels **(1957).**

they were sixty). The way Gable grew in stature on the screen can be observed by comparing *Red Dust* (1932) with its remake as *Mogambo* (1953). Even allowing for the advantage of having John Ford rather than Victor Fleming as the director, it is only in the later film that Gable comfortably fills the part of the great hunter, the man who is equally irresistable to broads like Jean Harlow and Ava Gardner and to ladies like Mary Astor and Grace Kelly.

The figure of the hunter is one of the standard adventure heroes, although more recent appearances have been cleaned up somewhat so that he is no longer in the deplorable business of just killing animals for fun or profit. Stewart Granger in *Harry Black* specializes in the socially useful task of shooting man-eating tigers. John Wayne in *Hatari* and Robert Mitchum in *Rampage* both catch their animals alive for sending to zoos. Indeed, in *Rampage* the old-style great hunter, Jack Hawkins, turns out to be the heavy, needing to kill animals for psychological reasons. It is Mitchum, the trapper, who now has the innate ability to make the right decisions – which used to be the prerogative of the hunter.

Mitchum, though, is the finest living exponent of the Adventurer, again in the pragmatic tradition of Bogart and Gable. Like them, he is an entirely unique performer. Although he has played psychopathic killers in *The Night Of The Hunter* and *Cape Fear*, most of his performances are without the neurotic edge that appears in Bogart when riled. And he doesn't exhibit the sort of well-bred gentlemanliness which runs through even Gable's most roguish parts – one

Clark Gable and Robert Ryan in
The Tall Men **(1955).**

The African Queen (1951) with
Katharine Hepburn.

HUMPHREY BOGART
with **Tim Holt** in
Treasure Of The Sierra Madre **(1948).**
The Big Sleep **(1946).**
Casablanca **(1942).**

135

THE WHITE HUNTER
Stewart Granger in
Henry Hathaway's *The Last Safari*.
John Wayne with Michele Giradon,
Elsa Martinelli and Hardy Kruger
in *Hatari!*
Clark Gable and Ava Gardner in
Mogambo.
Killers Of Kilimanjaro

can often envisage Gable as having been the blackish sheep of an exceedingly respectable bourgeois family. The Mitchum Adventurer combines awareness and intelligence with a drawling, almost sleepy relaxation. Possibly the essential Mitchum is to be found in Richard Fleischer's *Bandido* – he stands on the balcony of his Mexican hotel to observe the local war and lob a few hand grenades at the side which is going to pay him less for his services as a gun-runner. In his career, though, Mitchum has handled everything from the medical drama of Stanley Kramer's *Not As A Stranger* to light comedy – in Stanley Donen's *The Grass Is Greener*, he holds his own even against Cary Grant. In Otto Preminger's *River Of No Return*, he offers a portrayal of total integrity with all the conviction of a Joel McCrea or Randolph Scott. Perhaps because of his air of detachment, the typical Mitchum situation is one of being drawn into events. Some of his later parts go even further in making him an observer rather than a participant during much of the action – he is a war correspondent rather than a soldier in Edward Dmytryk's *Anzio*, and the person through whose eyes we observe Yul Brynner in Buzz Kulik's *Villa Rides*. But the pattern of being drawn into action rather than initiating it can be found in Mitchum movies right back in the 40s, like Jacques Tourneur's *Out Of The Past* and Don Siegel's *The Big Steal*. In Sheldon Reynolds' *Foreign Intrigue*, he ends up, quite without meaning to be, launched on a career of international espionage. Even in *Bandido*, in which he is clearly an adventurer by nature, he does not set out with the intention of fighting in the civil war, but gets caught up in the struggle of Gilbert Roland and his rebels against the repressive *federales*. Though he is far from being the man in the street, this movement towards increasing involvement makes him the representative of the audience in a way that figures of more obviously heroic stature – Peck or Wayne or Gary Cooper – cannot be. His screen persona differs from theirs in its apparent accessibility, without losing the essentially heroic dimension of a capacity for action, an ability to deal with situations as they arise.

In this very scanty survey of Adventurer stars, one more has to be mentioned because of the consistency with which he embodies a particular image. Charlton Heston differs from other adventure heroes in not appearing particularly sympathetic. He represents moral inflexibility. Set on a course of action, he is likely to pursue it rigidly to the end, no matter what disasters it may bring about. This has been his stance in films as diverse as *The Naked Jungle*, *El Cid* and *Major Dundee*, and one which seems well suited to the rather cold, harsh personality he projects on the screen.

The Adventurer stars dealt with here have all been male, which is reasonable enough as most Adventurer films are inherently male-centred. But there have been quite a number of Adventurer ladies, the most notably adventurous of whom has perhaps been the aggressive and resilient Susan Hayward who was at her best not in the Oscar-winning vein of *I Want To Live*, but roughing it out in the jungle in films like *White Witch Doctor*. She is quite capable of blasting Jack Elam with a rifle at the end of *Rawhide*, and in *The Snows Of Kilimanjaro* she is tough enough to send the witch doctor

ROBERT MITCHUM
with Martin Balsam and
Gregory Peck in *Cape Fear* **(1962).**

Not As A Stranger **with
Olivia de Havilland (1955).**

Villa Rides **(1968).**

The Big Steal **(1949).**

CHARLTON HESTON
as *Major Dundee* (1965).
El Cid (1961) with Sophia Loren.
The War Lord (1965).

packing and go to work with a knife on Gregory Peck who will otherwise die from the infection that is building up in him. She is the great outdoor actress – indoors, she is often a bit too much to take.

The leading Adventurer ladies, perhaps because their toughness does not square with the traditional notions of ladylike behaviour, are often at least partly on the side of the heavies. Barbara Stanwyck, for example, has always seemed more convincing when she is being heavy than when being sympathetic. The Stanwyck heroine is a wiry creature of terrier-like pugnacity; she has never looked out of place in man's clothes and doing a man's work. Allan Dwan's *Escape To Burma* found her jodhpured, managing a plantation complete with elephant teams. At the start of another Dwan movie, *Cattle Queen of Montana*, her father is killed in a cattle stampede that is not accidental and she sets out to run her spread with the cattle that remain and to find out who caused the stampede. Sometimes her self reliance goes beyond the limits of legality, as in *The Maverick Queen* or in Samuel Fuller's *Forty Guns*, where she was very much the boss, sitting at the head of the table, with twenty gunmen seated down either side. She was really a heavy in Rudolph Maté's *The Violent Men*. Here she was married to Edward G. Robinson, who was only half a cattle baron, having been shot up in a range war years earlier. However, Brian Keith, Robinson's younger brother, is whole at least in body and is in all sorts of cahoots with his sister-in-law. When Glenn Ford and the small ranchers strike back, setting fire to the baronial mansion, Robinson is caught upstairs with Stanwyck. As she escapes the flames, she pauses for a moment to snatch away his crutches and throw them into the holocaust below.

Ruth Roman, too, is at her best playing women of strong character if not necessarily of high morals. She contributed little as the token heroines of *Strangers On A Train* and *Bitter Victory*, making an impression only in meatier roles. At least on the surface she's a tough lady, often with a robust humour that allows her to survive trials that would break the spirit of someone less formidable. In André de Toth's *Tanganyika*, as a straight-laced Edwardian out in the jungle, she's game enough, when the going gets really clammy, to throw caution to the winds and discard her stays, which some passing chimpanzees pick up as playthings. In a couple of mid-50s westerns, Anthony Mann's *The Far Country* and Jacques Tourneur's *Great Day In The Morning*, she played ladies of dubious character who were associated with the heavy but in love with the hero, a situation resolved as usual in the movies by having her killed in the process of helping the good guy. In *Great Day In The Morning*, she was knifed by Raymond Burr, and in *The Far Country*, shot on behalf of John MacIntire; both were fancy-waistcoated gentlemen in the saloon business.

In *The Far Country*, we first see her on the river boat observing James Stewart being pursued by the crew, who want to lock him up on a murder charge. Her first line, from the door of her stateroom, is 'In here!' and her second is 'Hide in the bed' – which he does with spurs on. When the danger is past, she tells him as they sit up in bed that he'd look better with a shave. A very self-possessed customer,

ADVENTURER LADIES
Linda Darnell in *Forever Amber.*
Untamed — **Susan Hayward.**
Barbara Stanwyck, *The Maverick Queen*
Jeanne Moreau and Brigitte Bardot,
Viva Maria.
Ruth Roman.

MORE ADVENTUROUS LADIES:
Ava Gardner in *Mogambo* and
The Barefoot Contessa.
Jean Peters as *Anne Of The Indies.*

she operates in league with John MacIntire, the scoundrelly mayor of Skagway, running a saloon and clip joint called The Skagway Castle (her name is Castle). The toughness which allows her to run establishments like this and its Yukon branch, the Dawson Castle, is at least in part case-hardening (a recurring theme in Adventurer's dealings with the opposite sex is a major disillusionment at some time in the past). She trusted a man once, she tells Stewart, and it cost her a house in San Francisco and servants. 'Now ask me what a girl like me is doing in a dirty business like this.'

Jane Russell in *The Tall Men* **and as** *Montana Belle.*

In general, lady Adventurers are rather less than flawlessly pure – having been around tended to be seen in what might now be considered as a male chauvinist way – a qualification in men and a defect in women. Someone like Linda Darnell inhabited the hinterlands of moral ambivalence, rarely wholly bad or wholly good but enticingly in-between. In Otto Preminger's *Forever Amber* she was Amber, forerunner of the later, naughtier Angéliques and Carolines, an honest courtesan, a good mother and faithful in her fashion, though mightily put-upon by circumstances. Strong-willed and good in a crisis she was exactly the girl Cornel Wilde needed to lance his plague boil and pull him through when the population of London was being bubonically decimated. Among other female Adventurers, one might note Ava Gardner in *Mogambo,* Jane Russell in *The Tall Men* and Jean Peters in *Anne Of The Indies.* It is the broads rather than the ladies who flourish in the rugged surroundings of the adventure movie.

The adventure movie demands a directorial style as well as an acting style. The director who ought to be the master of the adventure movie is John Huston, but except perhaps in *The African Queen,* of which I have only the most distant recollection, the physical representation of adventure in his work comes only a poor second to his apparent ambition to be the cinema's answer to Ernest Hemingway. The great example of how not to shoot an adventure movie, though, comes from George Roy Hill in *Butch Cassidy And The Sundance Kid.* The camera style is so aggressively cute that it threatens to obscure the action which is the point of the movie – the great example of this is the opening robbery: it is shot entirely in huge sepia close-ups which gain nothing and obscure almost everything. The enormous success of the film at the box office only goes to show how supremely irrelevant the gratuitous artiness is – if ever there was a movie which sold entirely on the likeable personalities of its heroes, this is it. It is a good indication of the priorities in the popular cinema that, given the Paul Newman and Robert Redford characters plus a story line that offers the opportunity for memorable pieces of action, matters of camera style are of extraordinarily little relevance to most spectators. The greater is the pity, then, that the film did not provide the aesthetic satisfaction of a camera style which was of a piece with the action, rather than grafting on an alien display of visual fireworks.

The names of some of the most notable adventure directors have recurred throughout this book: Howard Hawks, Raoul Walsh, Richard Fleischer, Jacques Tourneur and Henry Hathaway. They

143

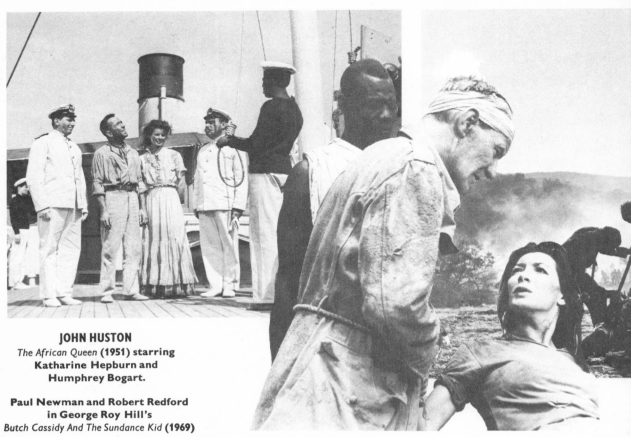

JOHN HUSTON
The African Queen **(1951) starring**
Katharine Hepburn and
Humphrey Bogart.

Paul Newman and Robert Redford
in George Roy Hill's
Butch Cassidy And The Sundance Kid **(1969)**

The Red Badge Of Courage **(1951).**
Trevor Howard in *Roots Of Heaven*
(1958).

are directors who are particularly good at handling the relationship between person and place, as V. F. Perkins has observed – among recent films, the parking lot shoot-out after the bank raid in Fleischer's *The New Centurions* offers an object lesson in staging action. Of the directors I have just mentioned, Fleischer is currently the busiest and most successful, but he is the one who has largely been passed over by the critical fashions that have brought recognition to the others. In staging and filming action, though, he has few equals – *The Vikings*, after all, is perhaps the most wholeheartedly enjoyable spectacular ever made. He seems to be particularly good at organizing enormous resources: the attack on Pearl Harbour in *Tora! Tora! Tora!* is as impressive a re-creation of a large-scale event as one could hope to see.

All the good action directors have an innate response to the medium that allows them to be at home when shooting outside the completely controllable environment of the studio. They are capable of reacting to their locations and taking advantage of the opportunities they offer. As Howard Hawks said of his methods in making *Hatari!*, 'You can't sit in an office and write what a rhino or any other animal is going to do.' They have an eye for things that are natural but striking – there is an extraordinary moment in Tourneur's *Way Of A Gaucho* when Gene Tierney wakes up to see Rory Calhoun standing on horseback so that he can see as far as possible across the flat expanse of the pampas.

All the adventure directors have styles that are confident without being obtrusive. They manage to achieve the maximum of effect with the minimum of fuss. Of all the directors, it is Howard Hawks who most completely embodies the ethics of the adventure movie. Hawks, who drove racing cars for a living and built aeroplanes before he was twenty, depicts a world where men prove themselves through mastery of their own actions. In any of his films, we know that the hero must, for his own satisfaction, complete whatever he has taken upon himself. 'There's three times in a man's life when he ought to yell at the moon,' says the cattle buyer at the end of *Red River*, 'when he gets married, when his kids come and when he finishes a job he was set on.'

Hawks' heroes are all professionals doing jobs – pilots, sheriffs, cattlemen, big game hunters: men who know their capabilities.

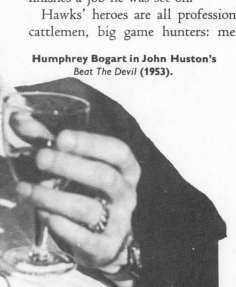

Humphrey Bogart in John Huston's
Beat The Devil **(1953).**

145

Henry Hathaway's
Lives Of A Bengal Lancer **(1935) with Gary Cooper and Franchot Tone.**
Jane Russell in *The Tall Men* **(1955), directed by Raoul Walsh.**
Raoul Walsh's *The World In His Arms* **(1952).**

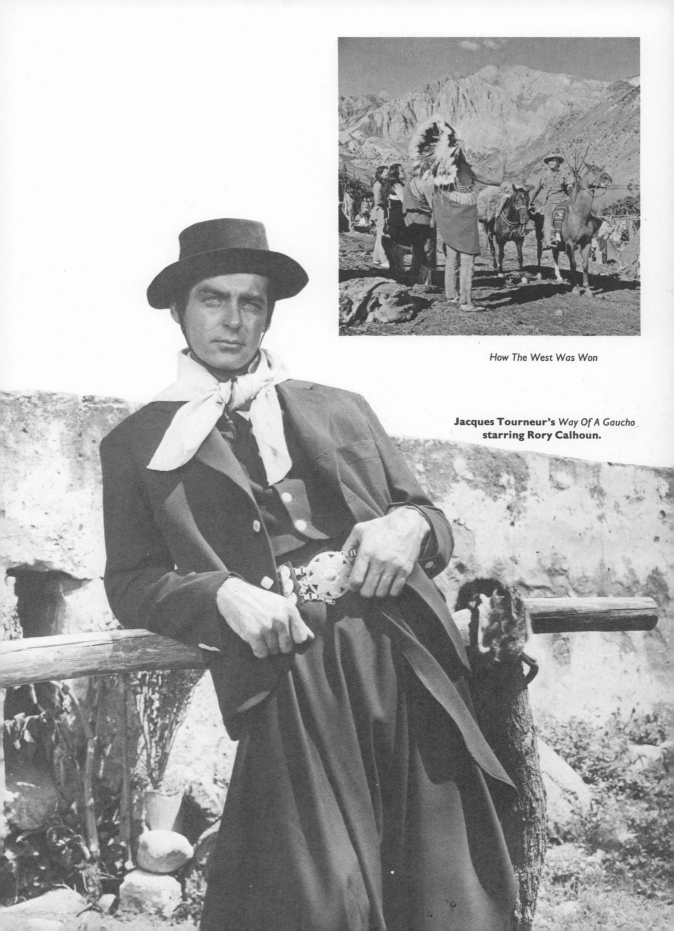

How The West Was Won

Jacques Tourneur's *Way Of A Gaucho*
starring Rory Calhoun.

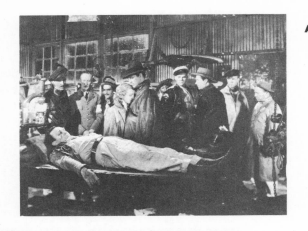

A scene from Howard Hawks' 1935 film, *Only Angels Have Wings.*

A scene from *Tora! Tora! Tora!* (1969).

James Mason and Peter Lukas in *20,000 Leagues Under The Sea* (1954).

Howard Hawks' *Red River* (1948).

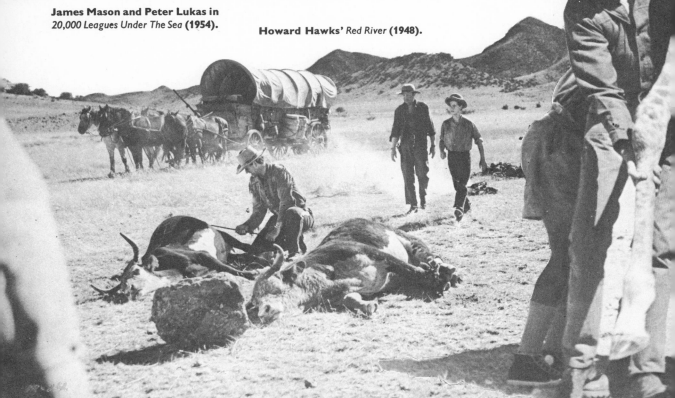

George C. Scott in *The New Centurions* **(1972).**
Hatari! **(1962) directed by Howard Hawks, with John Wayne and Valentin de Vargas.**

Their courage is the product of this self-knowledge. They know exactly what they can do with the available resources, expecting of others only what they know they can give. They assess their fellows only by the standards which have been tested by application to themselves. After a particularly hard day during the *Red River* cattle drive, John Wayne remarks to Montgomery Clift, 'The boys did all right'. Clift asks, 'Why don't you tell them so?' 'It's their job,' replies Wayne. There is no need of any heroics or self-congratulating gestures among men who can prove their professionalism through actions. The astonishing matter-of-factness of Hawks movies like *Only Angels Have Wings* and *Rio Bravo* comes from this absence of conspicuous valour or gun-twirling self-advertisement.

The attitude of Hawks heroes and consequently of the director himself is stoicism: there is no feeling of tragedy about the deaths in his movies. 'For me,' said Hawks, 'the best drama is one that deals with a man in danger.' For his heroes, the best jobs are exciting, and consequently dangerous. Men know they have a good chance of injury or death when flying aeroplanes, herding cattle, enforcing the law or catching wild animals. They accept the danger, and so do not make a fuss about the deaths. The epitaph repeatedly spoken by John Wayne in *Red River* is 'You brought nothing into this world and you've certainly taken nothing out.'

The professionalism of Hawks heroes is shared by the director himself. They get on with the job without any unnecessary nonsense. So does Hawks. He can say what he wants to through actions; the camera is there to capture the actions, not interpret them. Hawks uses his camera simply to do a job, just as his heroes would use a gun or a lasso. It is this pleasing fusion of form and content, of vision and expression that makes Hawks' best movies among the most satisfying experiences that the cinema has to offer.

INDEX

The Editors would like to express their gratitude to:
Ian Yeomans for the photographs on pp. 8,